Step by Step Guide to Embroidery

By Barbara Chandler

HAMLYN
London . New York . Sydney . Toronto

Emb.-A

Acknowledgements

I would like to thank Miss Eileen Bellamy and Mr. J. Clark of J. & P. Coats, Glasgow for their enthusiastic and imaginative assistance with this book. Instructions and designs for stitches have mainly been taken from J. & P. Coats' invaluable manual, '100 Embroidery Stitches'. Threads, fabrics, frames etc. for Chapter 1 were borrowed from The Needlewoman Shop, 146-148 Regent Street, London W1R 6BA. I should also like to thank Constance Howard for her encouragement, and the help of her students at Goldsmiths' College. Thank you to my mother, Mrs. Simpson, and to Su Gamson for their stalwart stitching, and to Anthony, Cathy, Xavier and Abigail for their patience and valuable criticism.

Published by
The Hamlyn Publishing Group Ltd
London . New York . Sydney . Toronto
Astronaut House, Feltham, Middlesex, England

Contents

Introduction 4

1. Basic Equipment 5

2. Your Guide to Stitches 10

3. Simple Ways With Stitches 17

4. A Sampler for the Seventies 24

5. Counting the Threads 26

6. Wool: It's Quick and Easy 38

7. Lettering for That Personal Touch 39

8. Special Stitch Effects 44

9. Counting on Canvas 46

10. Appliqué is Fun 57

11. Embroidery for Fashion Flair 64

12. Some Notes on Working Methods 69

13. Simple Motifs to Copy or Adapt 72

14. Finishing Off 74

15. Embroidery, Free Style 78

Index 80

Introduction

Ever since I completed my first line of straggling stem stitch, literally at my mother's knee, being only about six years old at the time, embroidery has continued to charm me.

Contrary to some opinions there is no great mystique about embroidery. Anyone, in a very short time, can master enough basic embroidery to get a reward out of all proportion to the small amount of initial effort involved. You will find that you can start almost immediately to put what you have learned into practice, as long as you keep your first efforts simple. You will find it very exciting to see just how effective simple patterns with simple stitches can be. This book provides the basic instructions you need to build up your stitching skill. It also aims to encourage you in your first ventures by presenting, along with groundwork instruction, several designs for you to copy or adapt.

There is no need for you to be doubtful about copying when you are beginning. The self-confidence, skill and experience required to create your own designs will come as time goes on. But it is very difficult for a beginner to know what the finished article will look like, and it is discouraging for first efforts to be bad ones through faults in design rather than faulty stitching. So don't be afraid to copy — or, even better, to adapt — until you feel ready to progress. You will find plenty of material in this book. Tackle a little bit at a time, concentrating on just a few pages or one particular item that inspires you. There is no pressing need for you to master everything: pick out what appeals for now and save the rest for later.

Embroidery is not an expensive pastime. You may well find all you need for a first attempt within your home already. Or for very small sums you can buy exciting new fabrics and threads. Whether for embroidery to add interest to something you already have, or for making embroidered articles from scratch, the ideas we feature were mostly designed especially for this book for you to copy or adapt. Some are ultra simple for beginners (or even children), others slightly more ambitious. They were created by artists and craftsmen/women, some professionally trained at art schools, others self-taught with a wealth of practical experience. Many were young; all were enthusiastic and I hope that their efforts and mine will provide sufficient impetus to start you stitching.

1 Basic Equipment

What do you need to start? It's so simple — just a needle, some thread and a piece of material (or a ready-made article), plus some idea of what you want to do. This chapter tells you about different types of needles, threads, fabric etc., and one or two other useful bits and pieces. The rest of the book helps with the ideas and stitching techniques.

FABRICS

After practising stitches on odd pieces of material, beginners may find it easiest to start on ready-made articles such as made-up napkins, traycloths, etc., or on clothes: the quick results on these are very encouraging. Just about any kind of fabric can be adorned with embroidery, unless you are working a design which depends for its effect of regularity on the accurate counting of threads (for example, cross stitch patterns, see Chapter 5).

In this case it is essential to have an *even-weave* cloth. This has the same number of vertical as horizontal threads per square inch. Embroidery shops sell special even-weave cotton

The same motif embroidered on three different even-weave fabrics

and linen cloths in lots of different colours, including vibrant modern shades of scarlet, lime, turquoise and so on. The delicacy of your final design will depend on the number of threads to an inch. Linens can have up to 34 threads to an inch, and they are more expensive than coarser kinds ranging from 19 threads per square inch. Cottons can range from 16 threads per square inch to 26 threads per square inch. Try and match your style of embroidery to the type of fabric you are using — a gay peasant design for a coarser fabric, for example.

Linen is a traditional fabric for embroidery and always looks good. It is available in many different colours, plus a pretty, natural, unbleached shade, and of course, snowy white. It wears and washes beautifully, so make sure the threads you are using are also washable and colour-fast. Cotton threads are a good choice. For working transfers or your own designs, it is possible to buy a range of traditional articles (trolley cloths, napkins, etc.) made up in cream and white linen.

Embroidery can also be worked on cotton fabrics of all kinds, from soft dress fabrics to sturdy denims. Don't exclude printed patterned fabrics from your embroidery programme. You can often work a simple pattern on top of the pattern to enhance the existing design, or you can appliqué motifs from patterned fabrics on to plain cloths.

Then there are richer fabrics such as velvet and silks for more luxurious effects. But avoid long-pile fabrics, because the depth of pile will cover up your stitches. Finer fabrics such as organdie, nylon, etc., can be used by the more ambitious for delicate embroidery. Materials with a drip dry finish are slippery and often non-yielding, making them tricky to stitch. Hundred-per-cent man-made fibres can pull out of shape.

It is amazing the difference that a careful wash and press can make to a triumphantly completed but slightly grubby-looking piece of embroidery (see notes on washing at end of Chapter 14). Colours come up with a lustre you may have forgotten existed! To avoid unnecessary soiling of the work, always try and wash your hands before starting, and keep the work from the outset in a strong bag (polythene will do) or box. Paper bags tend to disintegrate before the work is finished, odd skeins of thread get lost and work gets dirty.

It is sensible to shrink linen and cotton fabrics before starting work. Spread the fabric over a dampened piece of sheet or a tea-towel, taking care that both materials are completely flat. Fold the two together and enclose in a polythene bag for twelve hours but not any longer. Then remove the fabric and press with a fairly hot iron until thoroughly dry and crisp.

THREADS
There are lots of different kinds of threads available with which you can experiment.

Stranded cotton or six-strand floss is a good choice for beginners — it is shiny, the colour range is excellent, it is easy to work with and washes well. Use all six strands for very bold, large, simple designs making sure that the threads stay twisted together during work. For finer designs, separate the threads into the appropriate number — three is an economical choice, but for very fine work you can use just a single strand with effective delicacy.

Soft embroidery cotton is also an attractive thread with a thick matt, almost wool-like, finish. The colours are very alluring and you can use this for bold free-style work, or for counted thread designs.

Pearl cotton is twisted with a corded effect and shiny. Number 5 is thick, number 8 is thin, suitable for basic free-style stitches and counted thread designs.

Tapestry wool is a firm, well-twisted, matt woollen yarn, used as a single thread. Use it to add interest to cotton threads, checking that the colours are fast if your work is likely to need washing. This yarn is also excellent for working canvas embroideries.

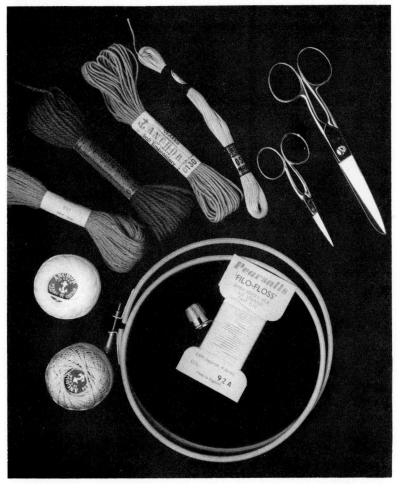

A selection of basic threads and equipment, including an embroidery ring

Crewel wool is a finer twisted matt wool with separable strands. **Silk** is gloriously soft and lustrous, but expensive. Use it for very special work.

These are just some of the possible threads — all sorts of other things can be used to add interest — metallic threads for example. If you are working large areas in a single colour, try and buy all your thread at one time as colours of different batches can differ slightly, and produce a disappointing change in tone. Store spare threads tidily so that you always have a good choice to hand for quick, spur-of-the-moment designs.

NEEDLES

It is worth taking some trouble to use the right sort of needles. Keep them in plentiful supply as they are the first thing to disappear — not necessarily lost, just borrowed by someone else for putting on a button. Bent needles make for uneven work: get rid of them. And a worn eye will fray your embroidery thread. A flannel book is recommended for storing needles.

Sharp needles are of medium length with a small eye and they are used for plain sewing, or for a single strand of stranded cotton.

Crewel needles, sometimes called embroidery needles, are the same as sharps but have a long eye. Common sizes range from 5 to 8 — the higher the number, the smaller the needle and its eye. A crewel number 7, for example, is suitable for three strands of stranded cotton, but you would need a number 5 with a larger eye for tapestry wool.

Chenille needles are a bit shorter than crewel needles, but just as sharp, and they have a longer eye, which makes them useful for wools and thicker threads (sizes 18 to 24).

Tapestry needles are exactly the same as chenille needles but with a blunt, rounded point. They are used for canvas work, or for counted thread work on coarse linen where no piercing power is needed. Common sizes are 20, 22 and 24, and remember once more that with all needles the larger the number the smaller the needle and eye. For tapestry wool you would need a size 20. For 3 strands of stranded cotton (working, say, a counted thread design on fine even-weave linen) you would need a size 24 tapestry needle.

Get to know your needles — they are your most basic and useful tools, but there are also some other handy pieces of equipment.

SCISSORS

Have two pairs if possible, and make it a household rule that they never leave your work-bag. Once the family get hold of them they will get blunted, or just disappear. A largish pair is handy for cutting fabric, and you will need a small pointed pair for trimming surplus fabric and cutting threads.

THIMBLES

Try and get used to working with a thimble if you can, because it protects your middle finger which may otherwise get dreadfully sore. A metal thimble is best and make sure it is light and fits well. Plastic thimbles are not strong enough.

EMBROIDERY FRAMES

Some small pieces of linen embroidery can be worked without a frame, but if the embroidery has areas of closely worked stitches, or complicated stitches, use a frame to prevent puckering and to keep the work flat and even. It is worth mentioning however, that many people hate frames, because the stitches require two movements and it slows the work down. Frames also tend to make you less flexible — your work is more difficult to carry around.

There are two types of frames. An embroidery ring or tambour is most commonly used for small pieces of work. Sizes range from about 4 inches to 10 inches diameter.

The ring usually consists of two wooden or metal rings, fitting closely one within the other, over which the fabric may be stretched tightly. The most useful type has a small screw on the larger ring for loosening or tightening it. This allows any thickness of fabric to be used.

The section of embroidery to be worked is placed over the smaller of the rings, the other ring being pressed down over the fabric on the smaller ring to hold the work taut. If a screw is attached, this should be tightened. The warp and weft threads of the fabric must be at right angles to each other within the ring. Sometimes the frame has a clamp so that it can be fixed to a table, or is mounted on a wooden stand to make a table-frame.

You should prepare your tambour frame by winding bias evenly all around the inside frame to cover the wood completely. This is to prevent damage to fabrics. Especially delicate fabrics can also be protected with a layer of tissue before pressing down the outside ring. You then cut away the tissue all round to within about a quarter of an inch of the ring so that you can work the fabric.

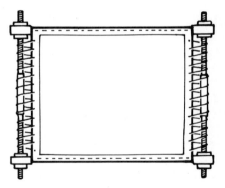

The second type of embroidery frame is square or rectangular and sometimes called a slate frame; this is especially suitable for canvas work, appliqué, and large pieces of embroidery. Square or rectangular frames have two horizontal bars with tape attached to them. The top and bottom edges of the embroidery fabric are attached to these tapes with over-sewing. The bars are then slotted on to two vertical rollers, and the frame is extended so that the work is taut and the four sides of the frame are fixed in place. The fabric is then attached to the side pieces. Thick material or canvas can be laced on directly, having first made a turning, but fine material will need to be strengthened with tape sewn along the edges.

2 Your Guide to Stitches

A knowledge of stitches is the key to turning the bleak lines of a transfer, diagram, or maybe your own sketch, into the rich texture of embroidery. Let's make one thing clear right at the beginning: you don't have to know all the stitches explained here before you can do successful work. Obviously the more stitches you can learn, the more varied are the effects you can create, but initially you can get some good results with a repertoire of say just five stitches.

Basic stitches fall very roughly into two main groups: stitches for outlining (e.g. back (2), stem (3)), and stitches for filling in solid areas (e.g. satin (11), long and short (12). Sometimes it is possible to fill in an area by using rows of outline stitches worked closely alongside each other, as you will see. There are also some slightly more elaborate stitches that make a pattern in their own right (e.g. herringbone, feather).

For the beginner's basic five, I would suggest back stitch (2), stem stitch (3), chain stitch (for heavy outlines) (22), satin stitch (11), and long and short stitch (12). Then try adding blanket stitches (19), French knots (28), feather stitch (20) and herringbone (18), and work up gradually from there.

Remember that the character of a stitch can be entirely altered by the size in which you work it and the type of thread you use. Of course these two points are related, because a thick wool is inevitably going to demand larger stitches than a fine single strand of stranded embroidery cotton.

Practising stitches can be a bit tedious. You will be impatient to get started on something usable or decorative. But your initial attempts won't succeed without some practice, so compromise by working a stitch sampler, which can grow into a decorative piece of embroidery in its own right. Or you could try working a perfect example of the stitches you like and mount them in a little book together with notes on how to do them, and how to use them, maybe with diagrams. This could be used for your own personal, quick, portable reference, or could make a useful present for a friend, maybe a child.

Well, then, here are some of the stitches from which you can choose. Do not be put off because there are so many: remember you can be selective to suit your fancy. A variety of stitches lends interest to your work.

1. Running stitch

Very easy this, depending for effect on its regularity. Pass the needle over and under the fabric, making the upper stitches of equal length. The under stitches should also be of equal length, but half the size or less of the upper stitches.

2. Backstitch

This gives an unbroken but very narrow outline. The correct way to work is right to left. Bring the thread through on the stitch line, then take a small backward stitch through the fabric. Bring the needle through again a little in front of the first stitch, take another stitch, inserting the needle at the point where it first came through. For whipped backstitch, whip over each backstitch without entering the fabric.

3. Stem stitch

This time work from left to right. This is a widely used stitch for flower stems, outlines etc., and it goes round curves very nicely, if you make the stitches small. Longer stitches give a finer line. Regular, slightly slanting stitches are produced along the line of the design. The thread always emerges on the left side of the previous stitch. This stitch can also be used as a filling, by working rows of stem stitch closely together within a shape until it is filled completely.

4. Laced running stitch

This turns running stitch, which is plain, into rather a decorative pattern, particularly if a contrasting colour is used for the lacing. Use a round-pointed needle for lacing to help you to avoid picking up any of the fabric. This would spoil the effect, which depends on an even, loose tension for the regular loops.

5. Pekinese stitch

Again, a transformation of a workaday outline by an extra process. Two colours can be used. Work back-stitch in the usual way and then interlace with a second thread. The stitch is shown open in the diagram but the loops should be pulled slightly when working.

6. Cable stitch

For more definite outlines. This stitch is worked from left to right. Fig. A — bring the thread through on the line of the design. Insert the needle a little to the right of the line and bring the needle out to the left midway along the length of the stitch, with the thread below the needle. Fig. B — work the next stitch in the same way but with the thread above the needle. Continue in this way, alternating the position of the thread. This stitch may also be worked on even-weave fabric.

7. Overcast stitch (or Trailing)

For a neat, ridged effect which looks like a fine cord. Good for delicate outlines but requires some patience. Bring the laid threads through at A and hold with the left thumb, then bring through the working thread at A and work small satin stitches closely over the laid threads, following the line of the design. The laid threads are taken through to the back of the fabric to finish.

8. Scroll stitch

Decorative enough to form a border. This stitch is worked from left to right. The working thread is looped to the right then back to the left on the fabric. Inside this loop the needle takes a small slanting stitch to the left under the line of the design, with the thread of the loop under the needle point. The thread is then pulled through. The stitches should be evenly spaced.

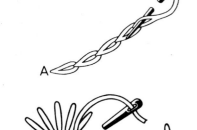

9. Split stitch

Bring the thread through at A and make a small stitch over the line of the design, piercing the working thread with the needle as shown in the diagram. Split stitch may be used as a filling where a fine flat surface is required. It looks very nice worked with thicker threads such as wool or soft embroidery cotton.

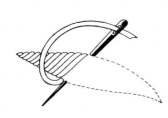

10. Straight stitch

Ultra simple this one, but useful in all sorts of designs. Here it is shown as single spaced stitches worked either in a regular or irregular manner. Sometimes the stitches are of varying size. The stitches should be neither too long nor too loose. This stitch may also be worked on even-weave fabric.

11. Satin stitch

Marvellous for filling in small shapes and if you can manage even tension with closely set stitches you will get a smooth pad of thread. It is often more effective to start stitches at an angle to the outline edge. Proceed with straight stitches worked closely together across the shape, as shown in the diagram. If desired, running stitch or chain stitch may be worked first to form a padding underneath. This gives a raised effect. Care must be taken to keep a good edge. Do not make the stitches too long, as they would then be liable to be pulled out of position.

12. Long and short stitch

This form of satin stitch is so named as the stitches are of varying lengths. It is often used to fill a shape which is too large or too irregular to be covered by satin stitch. It is also used to achieve a shaded effect. In the first row the stitches are alternately long and short and closely follow the outline of the shape. The stitches in the following rows are worked to achieve a smooth appearance. The diagram shows how a shaded effect may be obtained.

13. Flat stitch
A decorative filling stitch for flower petals, etc. Take a small stitch alternately on each side of the shape to be filled, with the point of the needle always emerging on the outside line of the shape. Two lines may be drawn down the centre of the shape as a guide for the size of the stitch. The stitches should be close together and fold into one another.

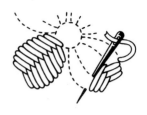

14. Fishbone stitch
Good for leaves, this stitch is useful for filling small shapes. Bring the thread through at A and make a small straight stitch along the centre line of the shape. Bring the thread through again at B and make a sloping stitch across the central line at the base of the first stitch. Bring the thread through at C and make a similar sloping stitch to overlap the previous stitch. Continue working alternately on each side until the shape is filled.

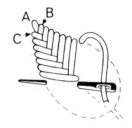

15. Open fishbone stitch
Bring the thread through at A and make a sloping stitch to B. Bring the thread through again at C and make another sloping stitch to D. Bring the thread through at E. Continue in this way until the shape is filled.

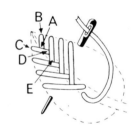

16. Leaf stitch
Gives the effect of leaf veins. Bring the thread through at A and make a sloping stitch to B. Bring the thread through at C and make a sloping stitch to D. Bring the thread through at E, then continue working alternate stitches on each side in this way until the shape is lightly filled. When this stitch is used there is usually an outline of stem stitch or chain stitch worked round the shape.

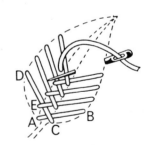

17. Roumanian stitch
A decorative filling with the effect of a whipped centre. Fig. A — bring the thread through at the top left of the shape, carry the thread across and take a stitch on the right side of the shape with the thread below the needle. Fig. B — take a stitch at the left side, thread above needle. These two movements are worked together until the shape is filled. Keep the stitches close together. The size of the centre crossing stitch can be varied to make a longer oblique stitch or a small straight stitch.

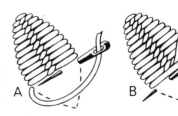

18. Herringbone stitch

Very pretty and quite easy to master, and makes a delightful little border edging. Bring the needle out on the lower line at the left side and insert on the upper line a little to the right, taking a small stitch to the left with thread below the needle. Next, insert the needle on the lower line a little to the right and take a small stitch to the left with the thread above the needle. These two movements are worked throughout. For the best effect the fabric lifted by the needle and the spaces between the stitches should be of equal size. This stitch can be laced with a matching or contrasting colour. Use a round pointed needle for lacing and do not pick up any of the fabric. Herringbone stitch may also be worked on even-weave fabric.

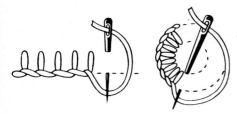

19. Blanket stitch and Buttonhole stitch

Again, simple but surprisingly effective. These stitches are worked in the same way — the difference being that in buttonhole stitch the stitches are close together. Bring the thread out on the lower line, insert the needle in position in the upper line, taking a straight downward stitch with the thread under the needle point. Pull up the stitch to form a loop and repeat. This stitch may also be worked on even-weave fabric.

20. Feather stitch

A pretty, lacy effect. Fig. A — bring the needle out at the top centre, hold the thread down with the left thumb, insert the needle a little to the right on the same level, and take a small stitch down to the centre, keeping the thread under the needle point. Next, insert the needle a little to the left on the same level and take a stitch to the centre, keeping the thread under the needle point. Work these two movements alternately. Fig. B — shows **Double feather stitch,** in which two stitches are taken to the right and left alternately.

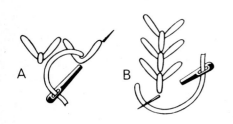

21. Fly stitch

Bring the thread through at the top left, hold it down with the left thumb, insert the needle to the right on the same level, a little distance from where the thread first emerged, and take a small stitch downwards to the centre with the thread below the needle. Pull through and insert the needle again below the stitch at the centre (A) and bring it through in position for the next stitch. This stitch may be worked singly or in horizontal rows (A) or vertically (B).

22. Chain stitch

Very good for bold outlines, and quite simple. Bring the thread out at the top of the line and hold it down with left thumb. Insert the needle where it last emerged and bring the point out a short distance away. Pull the thread through, keeping the working thread under the needle point.

23. Lazy daisy or Detached chain

So quick and simple for a pretty, flowered effect. Work in the same way as chain stitch (A), but fasten each loop at the foot with a small stitch (B). This stitch may be worked singly or in groups to form flower petals.

24. Open chain stitch

This stitch is shown worked in two parallel lines, but it may be used for shapes which vary in width. Bring the thread through at A and, holding the thread down with the left thumb, insert the needle at B. Bring the needle through at C, the required depth of the stitch. Leave the loop thus formed slightly loose. Insert the needle at D and, with the thread under the needle point, bring it through in readiness for the next stitch. Secure the last loop with a small stitch at each side.

25. Two-colour chain stitch

You will need a needle with a largish eye, and the effect is very intricate, achieved quite simply. This stitch is worked in the same way as chain stitch, but having two contrasting threads in the needle at the same time. When making the loops, pass one colour under the needle point and let the other colour lie on top. Pull through both threads. Work the next loop with the other colour under the needle point.

26. Cable chain stitch

Bring the thread through at A and hold it down with the left thumb. Pass the needle from right to left under the working thread, then twist the needle back over the working thread to the right and, still keeping the thread under the thumb, take a stitch of the required length. Pull thread through.

27. Zig-zag cable chain stitch

This stitch is a variation of ordinary cable chain stitch, each stitch being taken at right-angles to the previous stitch. Pull the twisted thread firmly round the needle before drawing the needle through the fabric.

28. French knots:

A good way of making small dots for flower stamens, etc. Bring the thread out at the required position, hold the thread down with the left thumb and encircle the thread twice with the needle as at A. Still holding the thread firmly, twist the needle back to the starting point and insert it close to where the thread first emerged (see arrow). Pull thread through to the back and secure for a single French knot, or pass on to the position of the next stitch as at B.

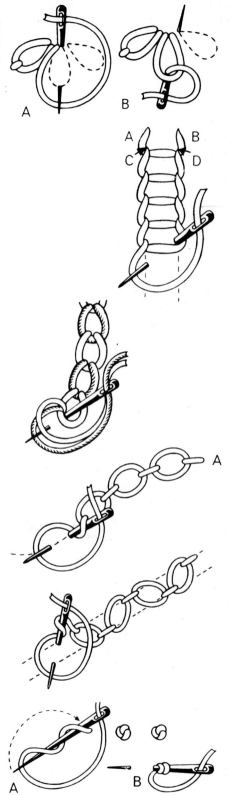

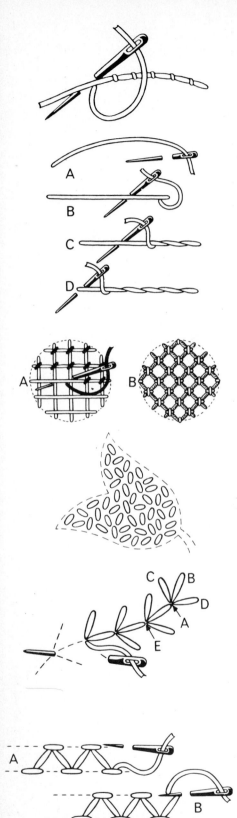

29. Couching
So pretty and easy, and very good for curved outlines, but not very suitable for repeated washing. Lay a thread along the line of the design and, with another thread, tie it down at even intervals with a small stitch into the fabric. The tying stitch can be of contrasting colour and type to the laid thread if desired.

30. Roumanian couching:
This form of couching is useful for filling in large spaces in which a flat, indefinite background is required. Bring the thread through on the left, carry the thread across the space to be filled and take a small stitch to the right with the thread above the needle (A). Take small stitches along the line at intervals, as in B and C, to the end of the laid thread, emerging in position for the next stitch (D).

31. Jacobean couching or Trellis
This stitch makes an attractive filling stitch for the centres of flowers or shapes where an open effect is required. It consists of long, evenly spaced stitches (laid threads) taken across the space horizontally and vertically (A) or diagonally (B); then the crossed threads are tied down at all intersecting points. The tying or couching stitch can be a small slanting stitch or cross stitch.

32. Seeding
This simple filling stitch is composed of small straight stitches of equal length, placed at random over the surface, as shown in the diagram.

33. Fern stitch
This stitch consists of three straight stitches of equal length, radiating from the same central point, A. Bring the thread through at A and make a straight stitch to B. Bring the thread through again at A and make another straight stitch to C. Repeat once more at D and bring the thread through at E to commence the next three radiating stitches. The central stitch follows the line of the design. This stitch may also be worked on even-weave fabric.

34. Chevron stitch
Bring the thread through on the lower line at the left side, insert the needle a little to the right on the same line, and take a small stitch to the left emerging half-way between the stitch being made. Next, insert the needle on the upper line a little to the right and take a small stitch to the left as at A. Insert the needle again on the same line a little to the right and take a small stitch to the left, emerging at the centre as at B. Work in this way alternately on the upper and lower lines. This stitch may also be worked on even-weave fabric.

16

3 Simple Ways With Stitches

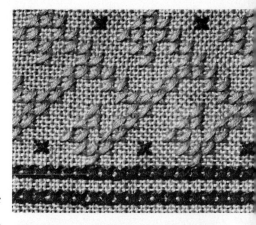

Now that you know how to work at least a few stitches, you will want to put them into practice as quickly as possible. There are lots of ways of doing this which can be worked in a spare couple of hours, or a free evening. Then as your mastery of stitches grows, you can start tackling more complicated projects. But don't scorn the simple designs. Not only are they ideal for beginners, but they frequently look stunning just because they are simple! Stitching borders is one of the easiest ways to begin. You can create borders from the stitches detailed in Chapter 2, or you can follow the two examples below. All numbers refer to Chapter 2.

Border 1
This railway wheel pattern is created from large loops of chain stitch (22), with smaller loops of back stitch (2). The small dots are French knots (28) with buttonhole stitch wheels (19). For notes on drawing curved lines see Chapter 12.

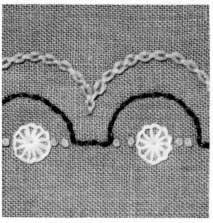

Border 2
This is an attractive fir tree pattern with tall trees of fern stitch (33) with extra back stitches at their base (2). The diamond pattern is a double line of chevron stitch (34) with a French knot (28) in each alternate centre. The bottom double lines are chain stitch (22).

Gingham border
Some fabrics lend themselves especially well to decoration with simple stitches. This strip of gingham, for example, would look great round the bottom of jeans. The bottom line of stitches is simple crosses in different colours. The middle line is straight stitch (10) following the line of squares. The top row is rick-rack braid caught down with single detached chain stitch (23).

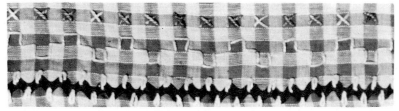

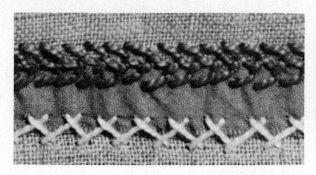

Above, left: border 1. Above, right: border 2

Braid borders

You can also use decorative stitches to hold down plain braids for pretty borders.

Border 1 has a top line of feather stitch (20) and a bottom line of herringbone (18).

Border 2. A wide braid is held in place along each edge with running stitch, whipped in a contrasting colour.

Progressing from stitching effects, you can incorporate simple pictorial motifs into your borders, possibly tracing suitable shapes out of books.

Leaf border

This is worked in three shades of green stranded cotton or six-strand floss, using three strands, with leaf outlines in fishbone stitch (14), and stems in satin stitch (11). The decorative base line is laced running stitch (4).

The leaf border

 The working of the butterfly motif opposite is described on page 22

Flower border

The central line is tapestry wool couched with stranded cotton (30). Stems are split stitch (9). Flower petals are lazy daisy (23) filled in with satin stitch (11), and the other flowers are groups of French knots (28). For notes on working out how to turn the corner of a border, see Chapter 12.

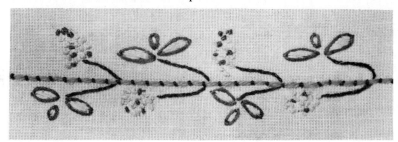

Daisy border

This is a pretty little flower border very suitable for children's clothes. Flower outlines are in chain stitch (22), with a single detached chain in the centre of each petal (23) and French knots (28) in the very centre. Stems are back stitch (2) and leaves are filled in with satin stitch (11). The dotted line in the diagram indicates the centre of the motif so that you match this to the centre of your work.

Suggested thread: Clarks Anchor Stranded cotton, or Coats and Clark six-strand floss, 2 strands for chain stitch, 3 strands for rest of work.

Alternative thread: Anchor Pearl Cotton No. 8, or pearl cotton equivalent.

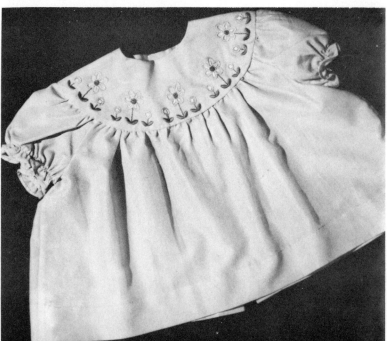

Table napkins

These have been designed so that the embroidery fills the folded area when the napkin is set out on a side plate. Design 1 is Art Deco inspired, and is simply worked in bold thick lines of stem stitch (3) using six strands of stranded cottons. Strong colours work best for this pattern, and we used a dark coloured linen.

Designs 2 and 3 are worked free-style within a circle (you can draw round the rim of a glass or use a compass). Design 2 is a beautifully simple sunburst, worked in running stitch (1) radiating from the centre. Design 3 is a more substantial sunburst using single lines of couching (30). Both these designs are intended for a napkin folded in a square and then into three. Design number 1 is for a napkin folded into a simple square.

Table napkin No. 1 (below) *is Art Deco inspired*

The decorative sunbursts (below, left) *for napkins No. 2 and No. 3*

21

Butterfly motif

You may feel ready now to progress to something a little more elaborate. The big butterfly motif looks rich and grand but in fact is incredibly simple to do. You can use it for any number of things, on the back of a shirt, for example, in the centre of a cushion, on a bag, or just for a picture. Trace off the outline, carefully following the instructions in Chapter 12, which also tells you how to enlarge or reduce the design. The whole pattern is then worked in chain stitch (22), rows and rows of tightly packed lines in six strands of cotton for filling in, and thinner black lines for outlining with three strands. In the circular spots, the line of the stitches goes round and round. Chain stitch is a very easy stitch to master, and once you have got the hang of it, you should find this butterfly very simple. There are many more motifs for you to copy or adapt in Chapter 13.

Greetings card

This attractive Valentine shows how an ordinary transfer of a very traditional flower pattern can be transformed into something original and unusual. The design was worked on silk in two strands of stranded cotton using stem stitch (3) for outline, sometimes singly, sometimes in double rows in contrasting colours. Flower petals are filled in with long and short stitch (12), and there are French knots (28) at the ends of the centre stamens.

The finished embroidery was pressed, and stuck on to a piece of thick card, using fabric glue at the edges only, and taking care to stretch the fabric as flat as possible.

Then a piece of flocked paper was cut to the same size as the card mount. A heart shape was cut out from its centre and the 'frame' stuck into place. For a less romantic card, an oval frame would have been just as effective.

The working for the Sampler for the 70's (opposite) *is described on page 25*

4 A Sampler for the Seventies

(Illustrated in colour on page 23.)

Samplers were the traditional way of teaching little girls to work their stitches, but that by no means lessens their appeal to big girls too. The earliest existing sampler is dated 1596, and they have remained popular to the present day. In Victorian times of course they were an essential part of every young lady's basic education, and were often used as a kind of final examination girls took before leaving school.

The simplest samplers are merely groups of different stitches arranged decoratively on a fabric, plain or coloured. Choose an even-weave fabric, as this will give you a chance to practice counted-thread as well as free-style stitches. You can plan a formal arrangement with a border (see Chapter 3) or cover an area at random. More advanced samplers incorporate letters and numbers: you could work the cross stitch alphabet in Chapter 7 as a sampler, adding a border from Chapter 5.

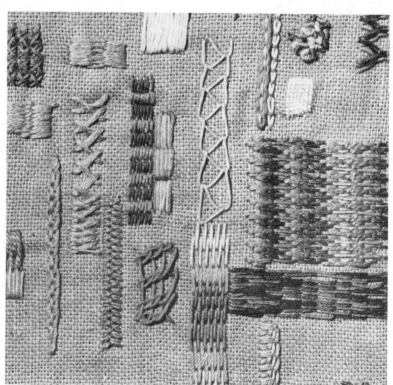

The simplest samplers are merely groups of different stitches arranged decoratively on a fabric, plain or coloured

We have had a modern sampler specially designed for this book, and besides making a decorative picture, it should give you a fair amount of stitch instruction and practice. Refer back to Chapter 2 for stitching methods.

The sampler in the photograph was worked very finely, the same size as the diagram we reproduce for tracing. But beginners may find it easier to enlarge the design, so that there is less necessity for very fine stitching. We suggest an enlargement of half as much again, which means that you will reproduce your design on a $\frac{3}{4}$ in. square grid. For notes on the tracing of designs and enlarging them, see Chapter 12.

Beginners will need to enlarge our outline design so that there is no necessity for very fine stitching. We suggest that their samplers are worked half as large again as our example which is illustrated same size on page 23. For notes on how to enlarge designs, see Chapter 12.

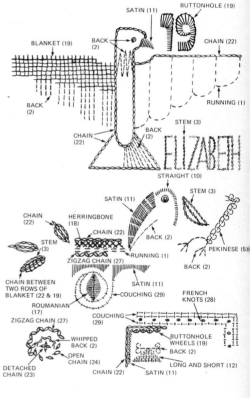

5 Counting the Threads

Counted-thread embroidery is precise, exact and rather different from the flowing curves and shapes you can make with the free-style stitches illustrated in Chapter 2. For this type of work, it is necessary literally to count the threads of the fabric in order to build up evenly-stitched designs which are, as a result, satisfyingly regular to the eye. Consequently a suitable even-weave fabric is generally used, with the same number of vertical threads as horizontal to every square inch. You will find there is a good choice, and the delicacy of the design will depend on the fineness of the fabric (see Chapter 1). Beginners are advised to stick to coarser fabrics where the number of threads is easier to count. Embroidery shops sell special cotton fabrics woven in blocks of threads.

The coarsest of these, which are rather stiff and unyielding, may have six blocks to an inch. Finer varieties may have 14 blocks to an inch. The squares of these provide easy guide lines for counted-thread work making them well-suited for beginners. You can also use even-weave linens, hessian (burlap), and hopsack and even try plain furnishing fabrics with a heavy regular weave. Designs can also be worked on printed fabric with a squared design, such as gingham.

Designs are perhaps more effective (though a little more difficult to work) when the fabric is less obviously made up of squares. There is a method for working counted-thread patterns on fabrics with too fine or irregular a weave for counting. For this you tack or baste a piece of fine canvas over the top of the fabric, using its squares as the guide for your design and sewing right through both. When you have finished you take out the tacking and draw out the threads of the canvas one by one. Choose fine canvas for fine designs and a larger size for coarser work. There is no need to use transfers, or outlines for counted-thread designs: patterns can be worked from charts, or you can work out your own design on squared graph paper, using crayons or felt-tip pens to experiment with different colours before you even thread a needle. Before starting to transfer a design to fabric, it is a good idea to work the centre of the fabric both ways with a line of basting or tacking stitches. These act as a guide for positioning the design.

Counted-thread work has always been popular in many parts of the world for gay folk embroidery and many designs

Instructions for this Figure Sampler are on page 33

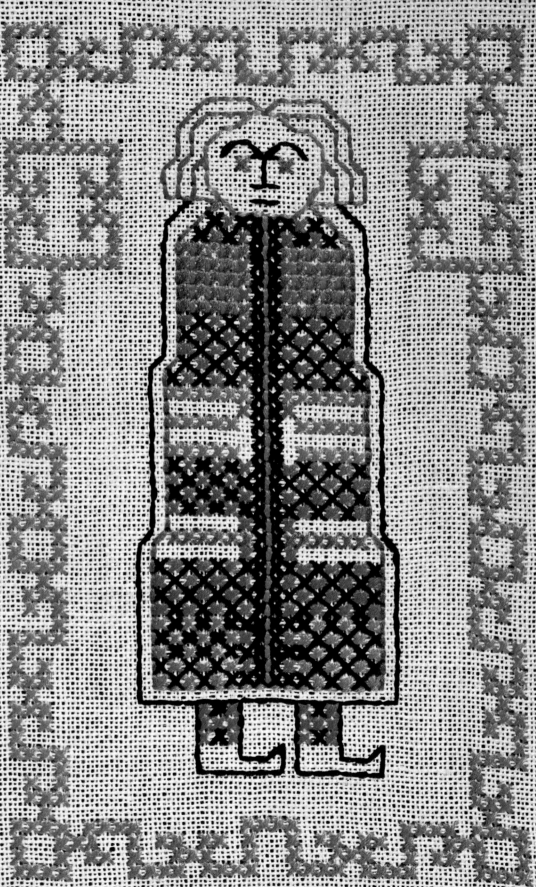

today retain this character. That is why they often look best worked in bold primary colours, or even one colour, possibly using coarse threads. Work with these progresses encouragingly quickly, particularly when the pattern repeats, so you can master it after a while without resorting to the chart. Many of the stitches described below are so decorative in themselves that they make a pattern in their own right, and once you have learnt the stitch you can work borders (or cover larger solid areas) for bags of all kinds, hand towels, table runners, mats, curtains, cushions and so on. Use a round-pointed tapestry needle so that it passes easily between the fabric threads.

COUNTED-THREAD STITCHES

Cross stitch

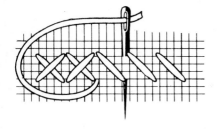

Everybody knows this one — very few children escape it! Don't let familiarity breed contempt. It's a beautiful stitch and needs quite a lot of care to look good. The stitches are worked over an equal number of threads each way of the fabric. Geometric designs are very suitable, but pictorial patterns are pretty, too. Beginners sometimes fail to understand that the *top half of each stitch must lie in the same direction,* otherwise the effect is messy.

The diagram shows how to keep an even tension, neither too tight nor too loose. Bring the needle out at the lower right-hand side, insert the needle four threads up and four threads to the left and bring out four threads down, thus forming a half cross stitch. Continue in this way to the end of the row. Complete the other half of the cross as shown. Cross stitch may be worked either from left to right, or from right to left.

Double cross stitch

Fig 1 — work a single cross stitch; then bring the needle out four threads down and two threads to the left. Fig 2 — insert

Detail of a table cloth pictorial border in cross stitch

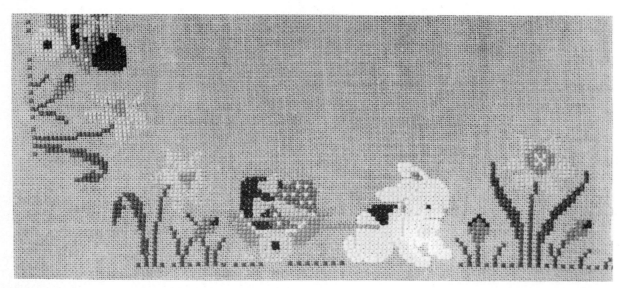

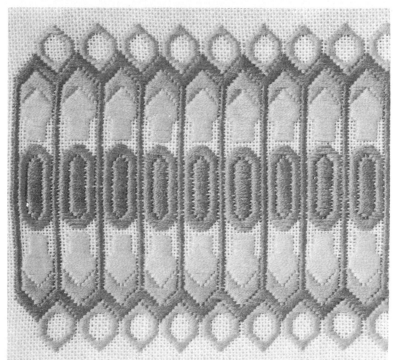

the needle four threads up and bring out two threads to the left and two threads down. Fig. 3 — insert the needle four threads to the right and bring out two threads down and four threads to the left, in readiness to commence the next stitch, or finish off at the back for a single double cross stitch.

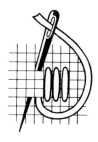

Long-legged cross stitch
This stitch differs from ordinary cross stitch in that it commences from left to right and one of the crossing stitches is worked over double the number of threads of the other stitch. Fig A — shows the method of working the stitch. Fig B — shows three stitches completed.

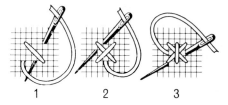

Satin stitch
This is an adaptation of free-style stitch number 11 and it is possible to build up very pleasing geometric shapes, making pictures or patterns. This stitch may be worked from right to left or left to right. The number of threads over which the stitches are worked may vary, depending upon the effect desired.

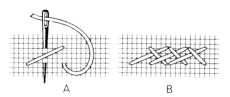

Back stitch
Bring the thread out at the right-hand side. Take a backward stitch over three threads, bringing the needle out three threads in front of the place where the thread first emerged. Continue in this way, working from right to left in the required direction.

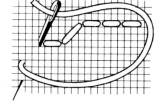

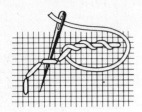

Whipped back stitch

This stitch is worked from right to left and is generally used in traditional Spanish Blackwork embroidery for outlining a design. Work back stitch first, then with another needle in the thread, whip over each back stitch without entering the fabric.

Holbein stitch

This stitch is sometimes called double running stitch. Working from right to left, work a row of running stitch over and under three threads of fabric, following the shape of the design. On the return journey, work in the same way from left to right filling in the spaces left in the first row. This stitch is used in Assisi traditional Italian formal embroidery designs to outline the cross stitch, but may also be used in other types of designs on even-weave fabric.

    The other stitches detailed below are used widely for drawn thread work, but of course depend for their effect on counting threads. They are good for filling in large areas and you can pull the relevant threads as tightly as you wish. These examples are in stranded cotton or six-stranded floss on linen with a 21 thread to the inch count, but you could make heavy duty items like bags, using the same stitches on a coarser, even-weave, using wool perhaps.

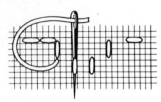

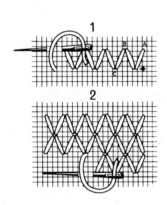

Wave stitch filling

This stitch is worked from right to left and can be worked as a filling as shown, or to form a border as shown in Fig 1.

    Fig. 1 — bring the thread through at the arrow; insert the needle at A (four threads up and two threads to the right), bring through at B (four threads to the left); insert at arrow, bring through at C (four threads to the left). Continue in this way to the end of the row. Fig 2 — turn the fabric round before commencing the second row. Work into the same holes as shown on the diagram to form diamond shapes. Pull all stitches firmly.

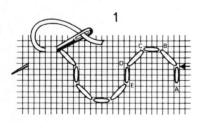

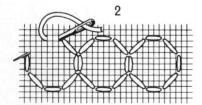

Ringed back stitch

This stitch is worked from right to left and can be used as a border or as a filling. Fig. 1 — bring the thread through at the arrow; insert the needle at A (three threads down), bring it through at B (six threads up and three threads to the left); insert at arrow, bring it through at C (three threads up and six threads to the left); insert the needle at B, bringing it through at D (three threads down and six to the left); insert it at C, bring it through at E (six threads down and three to the left). Continue making half rings of back stitch for the required length. Fig 2 — turn the fabric round for the second row and work in the same way to complete the rings. All connecting stitches are worked into the same holes.

The working of this modern version of a Jacobean-style motif is described on page 38

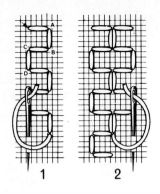

1   2

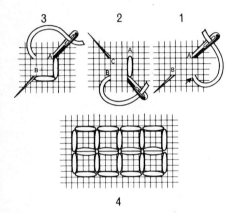

3   2   1

4

Honeycomb filling stitch

This filling stitch is worked from the top downwards. Fig. 1 — bring the thread through at the arrow; insert the needle at A (four threads to the right), bring through at B (four threads down), insert again at A, bring through at B; insert at C (four threads to the left), bring through at D (four threads down); insert again at C and bring through at D. Continue in this way for the length required. Turn the fabric round for the next and each following row and work in the same way. Where rows connect, the vertical stitches are worked into the same holes. All stitches should be pulled firmly. Fig 2 — shows two rows of stitching and how they form a filling.

Four sided stitch

This stitch is worked from right to left and can be used as a border or a filling. Fig. 1 — bring the thread through at the arrow; insert the needle at A (four threads up), bring it through at B (four threads down and four to the left); Fig. 2 — insert at the arrow, bring out at C (four threads up and four threads to the left of A); Fig. 3 — insert again at A and bring out at B. Continue in this way to the end of the row or close the end for a single four-sided stitch. For filling stitch: Fig. 4 — turn the fabric round for next and all following rows, and work in the same way. Pull all stitches firmly.

Cross stitch is particularly effective for building up geometric and pictorial designs. Although the basic stitch is so simple, the final effect is deceptively intricate, depending more on the ability to follow a chart carefully, and count threads accurately than on mastery of complicated stitching. The colour picture shows a cross stitch sampler motif designed expecially for this book. The finished work is the same size as the illustration. You could use it to make a small picture, in the centre of a cushion, or for the front of a bag or pencil sachet. The borders have a limitless potential. They can be used along the bottom of skirts, aprons, pockets, curtains, or around cushions, traycloths, table runners and so on.

INSTRUCTIONS FOR THE FIGURE SAMPLER
(Illustrated in colour on page 27)
Materials required
Clark's Anchor Stranded Cotton or corresponding colours in Coats and Clark's six-stranded floss: 2 skeins Rose Madder 057, 1 skein each of Violet 0100, Peacock Blue 0169 and Black 0403. Use 4 strands throughout. White even-weave embroidery linen, 21 threads to 1 in. 1 Milward 'Gold Seal' tapestry needle No. 24.

Method of working
The design is worked in cross stitch and back stitch over 3 threads of fabric. It is important that the upper half of all crosses lie in the same direction. Each background square on the diagram represents 3 threads of fabric.

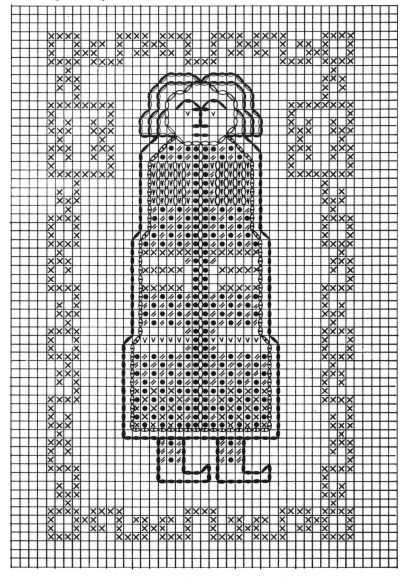

CROSS STITCH	BACK STITCH	
☒	◖	057
◿	◖	0100
☑	◖	0169
◉	◖	0403

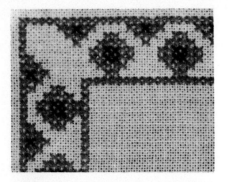

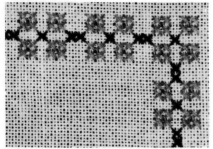

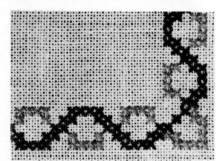

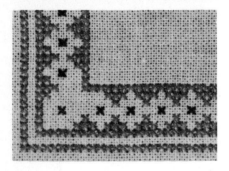

Four attractive cross stitch borders

Instructions for Cross Stitch Borders

These are worked in two colours, which should be strongly contrasting; we suggest a jade green with dramatic black, but you will have your own ideas.

Materials required

Clark's Anchor Stranded Cotton or corresponding colours in Coats and Clark's six-stranded floss: Jade 0188; Black 0403. Use 4 strands throughout. Even-weave fabric, 21 threads to 1 in. 1 Millward 'Gold Seal' tapestry needle No. 24.

Method of working

The designs are worked throughout in cross stitch over 3 threads of fabric and it is important that the upper half of all crosses lie in the same direction. Each background square on the diagram represents 3 threads of fabric.

KEY TO DIAGRAM

⊠ 0188
⊡ 0403

INSTRUCTIONS FOR THE TABLE RUNNER

Materials required

Clark's Anchor Stranded Cotton or corresponding colours in Coats and Clark's six-stranded floss: 4 skeins Chestnut 0352; 3 skeins Flame 0332. Use 6 strands throughout. $\frac{1}{2}$ yard gold even-weave embroidery linen, 20 threads to 1 in., 54 ins. wide. 1 Milward 'Gold Seal' tapestry needle No. 20.

Method of working

Cut a piece of fabric 14 ins. x 37$\frac{1}{2}$ ins. Mark the centre of the fabric lengthwise and widthwise with a line of basting or tacking stitches. The diagram gives A — half the centre section, and B — the border, the centres being indicated by blank arrows which should coincide with the basting stitches. Each background square on the diagram represents 3 threads of fabric each way. The design is worked throughout in cross stitch over 3 threads of fabric and it is important that the upper half of all crosses lie in the same direction. With one short side of the work facing you, commence section A at the small black arrow, 58 threads to the right and 3 threads down from crossed basting stitches, and work the design following diagram A and sign key for the embroidery. Commence the border centrally 11 ins. down from A and work, following diagram B and sign key. Turn fabric and work the other half to correspond. Press the embroidery on the wrong side, turn back $\frac{1}{2}$ in. hems, mitre corners and slipstitch.

Alternative thread: Clark's Anchor Pearl Cotton No. 8 (10 gram ball): 1 ball each Flame 0332 and Chestnut 0352, or a similar pearl cotton.

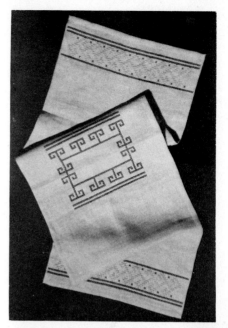

A cross stitch table runner and an enlarged detail of the border

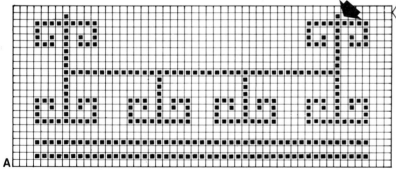

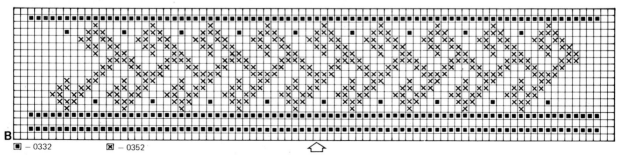

☐■ — 0332   ☒ — 0352

INSTRUCTIONS FOR CROSS STITCH APRON

Materials required

Clark's Anchor Stranded Cotton or corresponding colours in Coats and Clark's six-stranded floss: 8 skeins Flame 0335, 2 skeins each Buttercup 0298 and Black 0403. Use 4 strands throughout. $\frac{7}{8}$ yard white even-weave embroidery linen, 21 threads to 1 in., 59 ins. wide. 1 Milward 'Gold Seal' tapestry needle No. 24.

Method of working

Cut a piece from the linen $22\frac{3}{4}$ ins. x 37 ins. and mark the centre both ways with a line of basting or tacking stitches. The diagram gives A, the motif and B, a section of the border design. The blank arrow at A indicates the lengthwise basting stitches and the blank arrow at B indicates the width-wise basting stitches. The design is worked throughout in cross stitch over 3 threads of fabric and it is important that the upper stitches of all crosses lie in the same direction. Each background square on the diagram represents 3 threads of fabric. With one long side of the work facing you, commence the embroidery 30 threads to the left of the widthwise basting stitches and work motif A as given, following the diagram and sign key for the embroidery. Work motif A once more to the left and twice more to the right, spacing 60 threads apart. Commence border 123 threads down from crossed basting stitches, and work section B as given. Repeat B, 15 times more to the left. To complete the design, work the right-hand side to correspond. Press the embroidery on the wrong side.

Making up

Cut one piece from the remaining fabric $3\frac{1}{2}$ ins. x 22 ins. for the waistband, and two pieces 4 ins. x 33 ins. for the ties. Baste and stitch $\frac{3}{8}$ in. hems on each short side of the apron skirt. Baste and slipstitch a $1\frac{1}{2}$ in. hem at the lower edge. Make two rows of gathering stitches $\frac{1}{8}$ in. apart, $\frac{3}{8}$ in. from the top edge. Turn in the short edges of the waistband $\frac{1}{2}$ in. to the wrong side. Pull up gathers on the skirt to fit the waistband and with the right sides together, baste and machine-stitch the waistband to the skirt $\frac{1}{2}$ in. from the edge. Fold the waistband in half, lengthwise, to the wrong side, turn in the long edge $\frac{1}{2}$ in., and slipstitch in position to the line of machine stitching. Baste or tack and stitch $\frac{1}{4}$ in. hems on each long side and one short end of each tie. Pleat the raw ends to fit the open ends of the waistband. Insert the ties and sew in position.

Alternative thread: Clark's Anchor Pearl Cotton No. 8 (10 gram ball); 1 ball each Buttercup 0298, Flame 0335 and Black 0403 or similar colours in any number 8 pearl cotton.

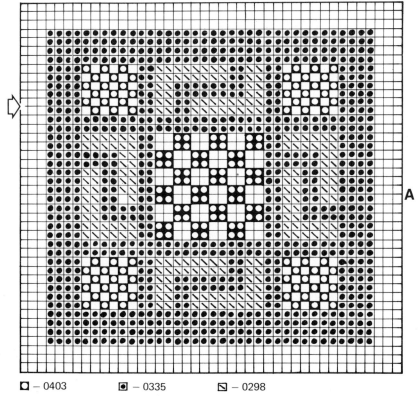

A

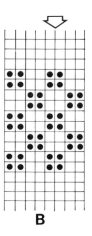

B

◻ – 0403   ◙ – 0335   ◩ – 0298

6 Wool:
It's Quick and Easy

(Illustrated in colour on page 31)

Embroidery in wool — sometimes called crewel work — was especially popular in Jacobean England, when intricate patterns of curving flowers, leaves and stems, butterflies and many other things in shaded colours were very fashionable. Wool is quick to work with and has a resulting texture and richness which is very satisfying. We have designed a modern motif for you to work in wool, based on the curving lines of Jacobean patterns, but very up-to-date nevertheless, with bright modern colouring. Note particularly the combination of turquoise and royal blue for the stem.

The stitches are ultra simple — mostly stem stitch (Chapter 2, 3) with some French knots (28— take thread 4 times round needle) and a little straight stitch (10). Our example is worked in tapestry wool. Different ways of using this motif are sketched below. Should you want to enlarge the motif, refer to Chapter 12. And remember of course you don't have to use the whole of this motif — you can adapt part of it for your own ideas. You can embroider the flower and the bee, singly, for example.

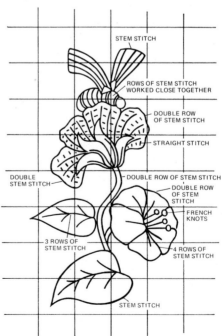

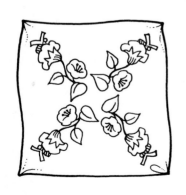

7 Lettering
for That Personal Touch

Embroidered letters can be decorative and also useful. They add a uniquely personal flavour to handkerchiefs, table napkins and clothes, also serving as a permanent identifying mark — very useful in large families or in schools and other institutions.

The tradition of embroidered letters is an old one, and you will find in embroidery shops and department stores a good selection of transfer alphabets in various well-known styles, e.g. italic, gothic and so on. These can be charming if worked neatly in, say, padded satin stitch as described below. Don't ignore these styles just because they are old-fashioned. That is part of their appeal.

You may however want to add more modern types of lettering to your clothes or linen, something more in keeping with today's trendy graphics. With this in mind, we reproduce three specially designed modern alphabets, and the illustrations suggest methods of stitching and application.

Embroidered letters make an attractive personal decoration for table napkins or on the collars of shirts

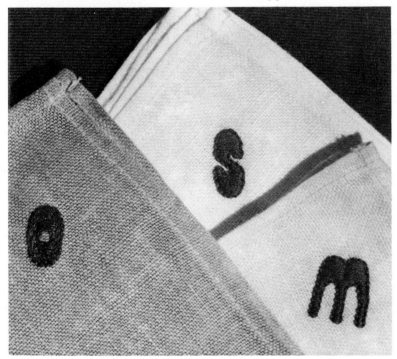

Names are quickly embroidered

THE ALPHABETS

Alphabet 1 is elegant and upright. The solid shapes can be filled in with satin stitch (Chapter 2, 11), or with finely worked rows of stem stitch (Chapter 2, 3). Alphabet 2 is more solid and chunky and can be worked quickly and effectively in outline (back stitch, splitstitch, stem stitch). See the shirt collar on p.39.

Both these alphabets are suitable for enlarging (see Chapter 12).

Giant initials for cushions or pillows, or the front of a T-shirt, can have a heavily embroidered outline (perhaps 2 or 3 rows of chain stitch, Chapter 2, 22) with possibly some extra decoration inside — a scattering of flowers in lazy daisy (Chapter 2, 23) maybe; or they could be appliquéd (see Chapter 10).

Alphabet 3 is intended more for adding whole names to linen bags, shoe-bags etc. It is quickly worked in chain stitch (Chapter 2, 22). When working names or messages, remember that letters should not be evenly spaced. If they are they will, funnily enough, look uneven. It is best to work out spacing by eye, juggling the letters until they look right.

ABCDEFG
HIJKLMN
OPQRSTU
VWXYZ
12345
67890;

A B C D E F G H
I J K L M N O P Q
R S T U V W X Y Z
1 2 3 4 5
6 7 8 9 0 ;

a b c d e f g h
i j k l m n o p q
r s t u v w x y z
1 2 3 4 5
6 7 8 9 0 ;

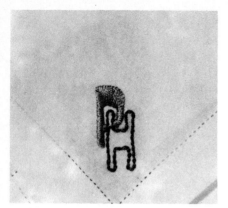

Letters on napkins and handkerchiefs should always be worked with the bases of the letters facing the corners

Monograms

We also show you a selection of monograms based on our alphabets: you can see the possibilities are limitless. There are no set rules; again it is a question of juggling the letters around, but often curves can be interlinked, or linked continuously, or letters can be fitted into each other, or uprights can be combined, with very pleasing and original effects. Obviously everybody's initials are not illustrated here, but the picture explains basic principles better than any words can. If you study it, you should find it fairly easy, using the basic alphabets, to work out your own monogram.

Some general tips

Letters on napkins, and handkerchiefs should always be worked with the base of the letter facing the corner.

Cross stitch lettering (alphabet 4) makes a cheerful, simple ornament for even-weave cloths (see Chapters 1 and 5). Our alphabet could be worked as a modern sampler in its own right, You can add one of the cross stitch borders illustrated in Chapter 5.

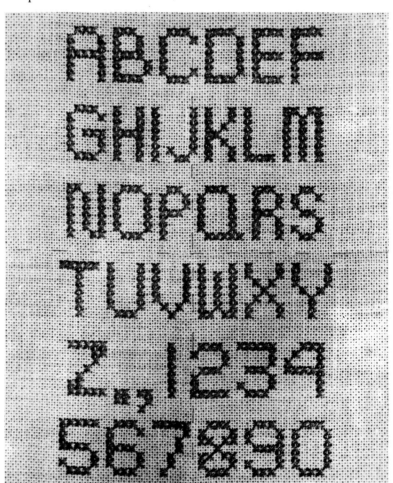

A cross stitch alphabet worked as a modern sampler

The traditional way

Very fine outlines can be worked by cording with overcast stitch as described in Chapter 2, 7. The fine line produced can be used for the thin parts of traditional lettering styles, while the thick parts are filled in solid with padded satin stitch. This has an atttractive raised effect and depends on an extra base of padding stitches completely covered by a top layer. Use a slightly heavier thread for the base padding. Outline the thick parts of the letter in fine running or chain stitches, working just inside your guide line. Fill in the area with chain stitch or running stitch. Thread your needle with a finer thread (say 2 or 3 strands of stranded cotton or six-strand floss) and work over the padding in satin stitch (Chapter 2, 11) placing the needle exactly through the fabric right on the stamped outline. Each stitch must be of an even length and placed just a thread apart each time. The closer the stitches are placed the smoother the finished effect. For straight sections of letters, keep stitches at right angles to the outline. Turn the stitches gradually to follow curves in letters such as a C or S. In a corner, such as you get in an E or an M, the turn may be more abrupt.

You will find a small tambour embroidery frame very useful for working lettering, providing the letter is not too near the edge of the article to be embroidered, in which case you will have to stitch the embroidery fabric to a muslin backing to leave room round it.

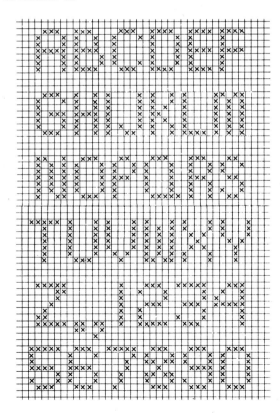

8 Special Stitch Effects

Some stitches are so flamboyantly decorative that designs need to be planned around them for maximum effect. Nevertheless, these stitches make a design statement in their own right, and mastery of any one of them will give you excitingly different edgings, borders etc. for all sorts of different articles.

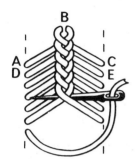

Vandyke stitch
Bring the thread through at A. Take a small horizontal stitch at B and insert the needle at C. Bring the thread through at D. Without piercing the fabric, pass the needle under the crossed threads at B and insert at E. Do not pull the stitches too tightly, otherwise the regularity of the centre plait will be lost.

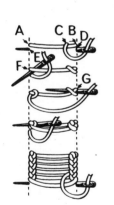

Ladder stitch
This stitch may be used to fill shapes of varying widths, but it is shown worked between parallel lines. Bring the thread through at A, insert the needle at B and bring it out at C. Insert again at D and bring out at E. Pass the needle under the first stitch at F and through the double stitch at G. Continue in this way, the needle passing under two stitches at each side to form the plaited edge.

Interlacing stitch
The foundation of this border is a double row of herringbone stitch worked in two journeys, with the stitches inter-twined. The first row of herringbone stitch is shown in medium tone on the diagram. In working the rows of herringbone stitch for the interlacing, there is a slight change in the usual method. In the top stitch the needle is passed under the working thread in each case instead of over, and attention should be paid to the alternate crossing of the threads when working the second row. Do not work this foundation tightly, as the interlacing thread tends to draw the stitches together. When the rows of herringbone stitch are worked, bring the thread for the surface interlacing through at A and follow the diagram closely. When the end of the row is reached, lace the thread round the last cross in the centre and work back in a similar fashion along the lower half of the foundation. The last two crosses on the diagram have been left unlaced so that the construction of the herringbone stitch may be seen clearly.

Interlaced Band

This stitch is composed of two rows of back stitch with an interlacing. Work two parallel rows of back stitch (as shown at the top of the diagram) having the rows approximately $\frac{1}{2}$ in. — $\frac{3}{4}$ in. apart, with the stitches worked as on the diagram, i.e. the end of one stitch is directly in line with the centre of the opposite stitch. Bring a matching or contrasting thread through at A and interlace it through every stitch.

Maltese Cross

This is worked in a similar way to interlacing stitch. The intertwining of the herringbone stitch must be worked accurately, otherwise the interlacing cannot be achieved. Bring the thread through at A and take a stitch from B to C. Carry the thread from C to D and take a stitch from D to E. Continue in this way following diagram 1 until the foundation is complete. Diagram 2 shows the method of interlacing, which commences at F. Diagram 3 shows the complete motif.

Portuguese Border Stitch

Work the required number of foundation bars which are evenly spaced horizontal straight stitches. Bring the thread through at A, with the working thread to the left of the needle, carry it over and under the first two bars, then over the first two bars and under the second bar only, without piercing the fabric. The thread is now in position B to commence the second pair of stitches. Continue working to the top of the row. Bring a new thread through at C and proceed in exactly the same way, but with the working thread to the right of the needle.

Raised chain band

Work the required number of foundation bars, which are fairly closely spaced horizontal straight stitches. Bring the thread through at A, then pass the needle upwards under the centre of the first bar and to the left of A. With the thread under the needle, pass the needle downwards to the right of A and pull up the chain loop thus formed.

Striped Woven Band

Work the required number of foundation bars, which are evenly spaced horizontal straight stitches. Thread two needles with contrasting threads and bring them through the fabric to lie side by side at A, the light thread on the left side. Pass the light thread under the first straight stitch and leave it lying. Take dark thread over the first straight stitch and under second straight stitch and also under the light thread. Leave dark thread lying, and pass the light thread over the second straight stitch, under third straight stitch and also under the dark thread. Continue to the end of the border. Begin each following row from the top.

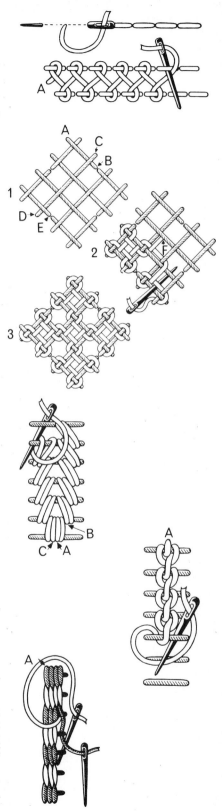

45

9 Counting on Canvas

Canvas-work (needlepoint) is an extension of counted-thread embroidery; many of the stitches can be used for either (including the cross stitch family), but embroidery on canvas, because of the sturdy nature of the basic material, plus the fact the usual working thread is hard-wearing wool, becomes very suitable for articles that are going to receive a fair amount of tough wear: chair seats, for example, or bags and belts. Other threads besides wool can, of course, be used, but the idea usually is to cover the whole surface of the canvas. There is no need for canvas designs to be functional: people make the most beautiful pictures and wall hangings using stitches on canvas. This chapter is intended to introduce you to the basic stitches, plus giving a selection of the more decorative techniques and some ideas for things you can make.

Choosing the canvas

Two types of canvas are available, double-thread (better for cross stitches) and single thread. The density of double-thread canvas is determined by the number of holes to the inch, and number 10 is suitable for most kinds of furnishing work. Single thread canvas is measured by the number of threads to the inch, and comes in much finer qualities with up to 24 threads to the inch for very delicate work. Thus, with canvas-work, designs can always be enlarged or reduced simply by adjusting the gauge of the canvas.

The threads to use

Basic threads are crewel wool, a fine 2 ply separable yarn, and tapestry wool, a single 4 ply thread. Other kinds of threads can add interest and different textures to your work. Use a blunt-ended tapestry needle (see Chapter 1). In general you can use one strand of crewel wool on single thread canvas with 18 to 24 threads to the inch, two strands of crewel wool on single thread canvas with 16 threads to the inch, and tapestry wool on double thread canvas with 10 holes to the inch.

Knitting wool is not suitable for canvas work because it is not twisted firmly enough and wears thin when repeatedly pulled through the canvas.

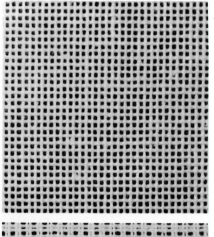
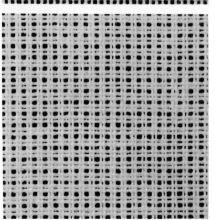

Single-thread canvas (top) and double-thread canvas

Working on a frame

Small pieces of canvas work can be worked without a frame but a square or rectangular frame may be useful for larger projects (see Chapter 1). There are various types of square or rectangular frames and your needlework shop will advise on the best one for your needs. Mount the canvas on the frame in the following manner:

A. Mark the centre of the canvas both ways with a line of basting or tacking stitches and mark the centre of the rollers with a pencil.

B. Fold down $\frac{1}{2}$ in. of the cut edge of the canvas and sew securely to the tape on the rollers which lie at the top and bottom of the frame. If required, turn in the selvedge sides to fit the tapes. The centre pencil marks should be matched to the centre basting stitches on the canvas when sewing the canvas to the tape.

C. Wind the surplus canvas round the rollers, assemble the frame and adjust the screws so that the canvas is stretched taut from top to bottom.

D. The sides of the canvas are now laced round the laths with fine string or four strands of button thread.

Useful hints

When working on single or double thread canvas, bear in mind the following points:

Buy all wool at one time, particularly the wool for the background, to make sure the colour does not vary.

Leave 2-3 ins. of unworked canvas all round in order to facilitate mounting. Work to an even tension, not pulling the wool too tightly. This is particularly necessary when working on double-thread canvas, otherwise the threads of the canvas will not be completely covered.

Keep the back of the work smooth and free from knots.

Never have more than 18 ins. of tapestry wool in the needle.

Make every stitch in two movements.

Blocking and cleaning

After the work is completed, your canvas may be distorted and stretching may be required. Allow at least two inches of canvas all round the finished work for stretching. Never iron canvas work, as this will flatten the stitches. Instead take a large piece of wood or insulation board and cover it with several sheets of blotting paper (white). Then use cold water to dampen the back of your canvas, and place the piece of work face down on the board, pulling it gently into shape and fastening it down with drawing pins. Repeat the dampening process and leave it to dry naturally, which will take at least a day. A piece of embroidery worked on canvas must always be dry cleaned as the use of water would soften the canvas.

STITCHES

Tent stitch
The basic stitch for canvas work is tent stitch, best worked on single thread canvas across the intersection of one weft and one warp thread. Here are two different ways of working tent stitch.

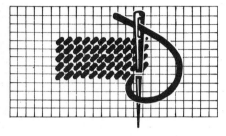

Method 1 (known as half-cross stitch). Start at upper left corner of canvas. Bring the needle to the front of the canvas at point that will be the bottom of the first stitch. The needle is in a vertical position when making stitch. Always work from left to right, and turn the work around for the return row. Catch the yarn ends in finished work on the back.

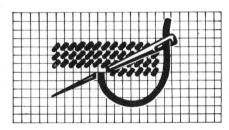

Method 2 (sometimes known as continental stitch). Start the design at the upper right corner. To begin, keep back an inch of yarn on its wrong side and work over this end. All other strands may be started and finished by running them through the wrong side of the finished work. Details 1 and 2 show placement and direction of the needle; turn work around for the return row. Always work from right to left. Finish your design first and then fill in the background. This uses more wool than Method 1 but it covers the canvas both front and back and makes for a more decorative surface. Petit Point is this stitch worked on canvas, 20 threads to the inch or smaller.

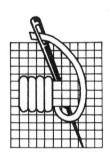

Upright gobelin stitch
This is also a useful basic stitch. Working from bottom to top, take upright stitch over three or four horizontal threads. Continue across from left to right, placing stitches immediately next to one another. Rows are begun in same way as for tent stitch, above.

Many canvas stitches are so decorative that they can be used on their own to cover areas for bags, cushions, chair seats, etc., without the introduction of any motif. This is a very relaxing way of doing embroidery, albeit repetitive.

Here are some of the more decorative stitches.

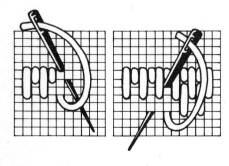

Gobelin filling stitch (also known as Bricking)
This stitch is worked in rows alternately from left to right. The first row consists of long and short stitches over four and two threads. The second row consists of straight stitches which are worked over four threads and fit evenly into the preceding row. Continue working in this way to the last row, which is worked to correspond with the first.

Chequer stitch

This stitch is used for filling large areas to give a woven fabric effect. The pattern consists of alternating squares of satin stitch and tent stitch, each square worked over four horizontal and four vertical threads of canvas. The easiest method of working this stitch is to work the squares in diagonal rows commencing at the upper left-hand corner.

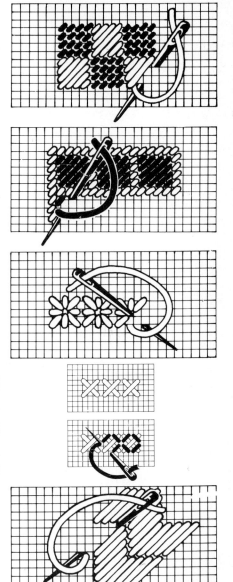

Scottish stitch

This stitch consists of regular squares of slanted satin stitch worked over three threads, divided by single lines of tent stitch.

Star stitch

This stitch forms a square over four horizontal and four vertical threads of canvas. It consists of eight straight stitches over two canvas threads, each worked from the outer edge into the same central hole as shown in the diagram.

Rice stitch

This stitch can be worked in two contrasting threads, a thick thread for the large cross stitch which forms the foundation of the work, and a fine thread for the small straight stitch which goes on top. Step 1 is to cover the area required with cross stitch (see Chapter 5), worked over four threads each way of the canvas. Step 2 is to work small diagonal straight stitches over the corners of each cross stitch. These threads are at right angles to the basic cross stitches, and are worked over two threads each way of the canvas.

Byzantine stitch

Forms an attractive zig-zag pattern. Work diagonal stitches over four threads of canvas, four across and four down.

Florentine stitch

This is of ancient origin and was generally used for covering cushions and chair seats. The distinctive zig-zag pattern is its special striking feature. Traditionally, several shades of one colour are used for a graduated effect, and the work consists of perpendicular stitches in a variety of possible combinations, one of which is shown here.

All stitches are worked over three threads of canvas. Use the chart to establish the basic zig-zag pattern, then fill in with rows in contrasting or related colours, following the same pattern of stitches.

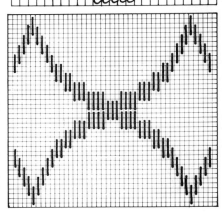

Spring

1. Pale mauve	14. Off-white
2. Mid-blue	15. Pale cream
3. Pale blue	16. Cream
4. Navy blue	17. Tan
5. Aquamarine	18. Rose pink
6. Mid-green	19. Pale pink
7. Dark green	20. White
8. Gold	21. Deep rose-pink
9. Deep yellow	22. Beige
10. Mid-yellow	23. Mid-grey
11. Pale yellow	24. Maroon
12. Pale green	25. Fawn
13. Pale turquoise	26. Chocolate brown
	27. Lime green

Summer

1. Yellow	8. Dark brown
2. Pale blue	9. Dark grey
3. Navy blue	10. Pale grey
4. Tan	11. Beige
5. Mid-green	12. Gold
6. White	13. Crimson
7. Emerald green	14. Orange
	15. Scarlet

Autumn

1. Tan	12. Royal blue
2. Fawn	13, 14, 15, 16 and 17.
3. Cream	Graded shades
4, 5, 6 and 7.	from mid-blue
Graded shades	shading to grey
of mid-brown	18. Aquamarine
8. Purple	19. Dark brown
9. Deep purple	20. Mid-green
10. Maroon	21. Lime green
11. Bright blue	22. Orange

Winter

1. Pale blue	11. Aquamarine
2. Deep purple	12. Light navy
3. Maroon	13. Dark navy
4. Dull mauve	14. Dark blue-green
5. Pale grey	15. Dark fir-green
6. Mid-grey	16. Chocolate brown
7. Mid-blue	17. Tan
8. Turquoise	18. Light tan
9. Royal blue	19. Mid-brown
10. Dark grey	20. White

Making a start

Start practising canvas-work with tent stitch. We have designed some little animals for you to copy to make your work more decorative. Then move to the other more elaborate stitches, maybe building up a stitch sampler as you go along. A sampler of this kind can be a decorative piece of embroidery even when the original intention was merely to practise stitches.

Four-seasons panels

Designed by Tony Chiltern-Cooper. These four charming little designs represent the four seasons. You can work each one individually, to made canvas-work pictures, or you can work a block of four on the same piece of canvas to make a cushion cover. Single panels also make an attractive front for a bag or large purse.

Each panel, worked over single thread canvas, 16 threads to the inch, measures 6 in. by $4\frac{1}{4}$ in. But the designs can be enlarged by using canvas of a coarser gauge.

The panels are worked in soft embroidery cotton. The basic stitch is upright gobelin over three threads of canvas, but the stitch length varies for the detailing. Use the diagrams as a guide.

Before you start, you can, if you wish, mark out the outlines of the design on your canvas, using a fine ball-point pen, and copying the squared diagram exactly.

Colour guide for the panels

The numbers on the following lists correspond to the numbers on the diagrams, and are intended as a guide to colours. Summer is the easiest panel for a beginner, because it has the fewest colours. The effect of the other three designs depends to a considerable extent on the rows of closely graded shades of colour for the backgrounds, as indicated on the colour lists. Beginners, however, might find it easier to work the backgrounds in one solid colour. In this case, suitable background colours would be: Spring, bright yellow; Autumn, royal blue; and Winter, mid-blue.

It is suggested that you use soft embroidery cotton because of the good range of closely graded colours available. But you could also use two strands of crewel wool.

On the opposite page are two of the Four Seasons panels, which can be used in any number of combinations

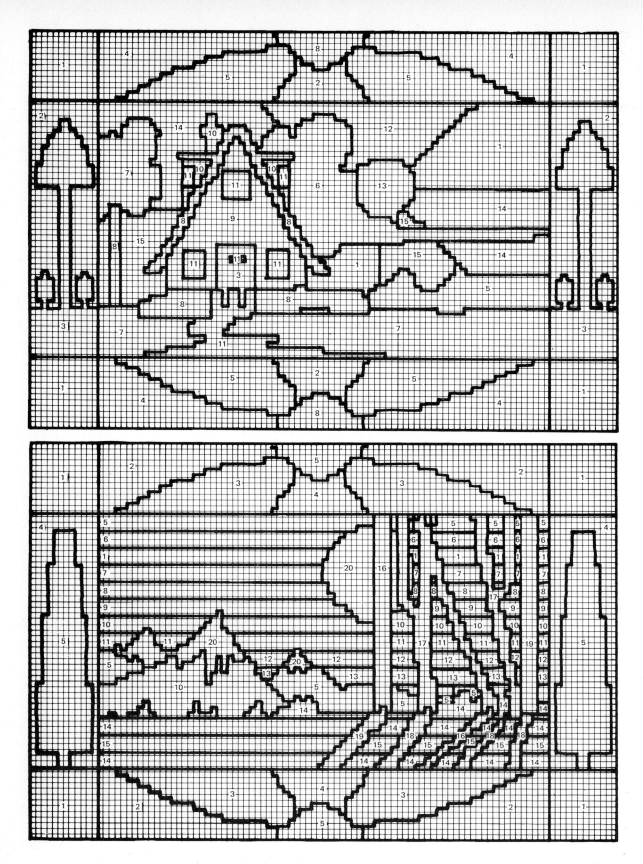

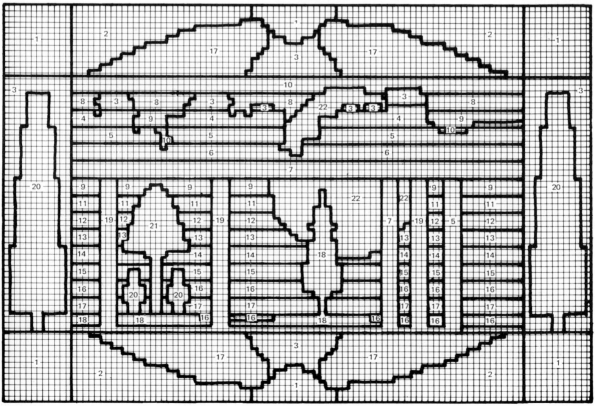

Instructions for making the picture opposite are on pages 65 and 66

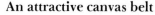

An attractive canvas belt

Designed by Su Gamson. This is worked, in two strands of crewel wool, in white, black and three shades of grey on single thread canvas, 16 threads to the inch. The stitches involved are tent stitch over two threads, and petit point over one thread, blocks of satin stitch over four threads, and blocks of upright gobelin stitch over four threads. Follow the diagram as a guide to the stitches and their direction; follow the photograph as a guide to the colouring.

You can see that this design falls into three sections. Section A can be used merely to begin and end your belt; or you can take this design and work it as a single square for a pincushion, or as a series of squares for a cushion with a squared patchwork effect. For your belt you can either work a complete repeat of section B and C, or merely repeat either section B or section C, which would be simpler to start with.

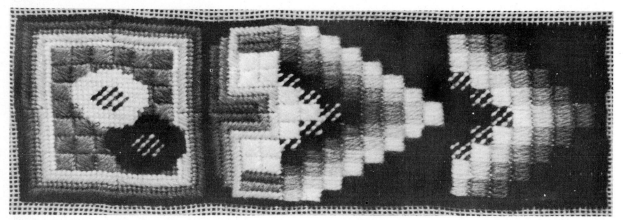

Details of the canvas belt, worked in crewel wool

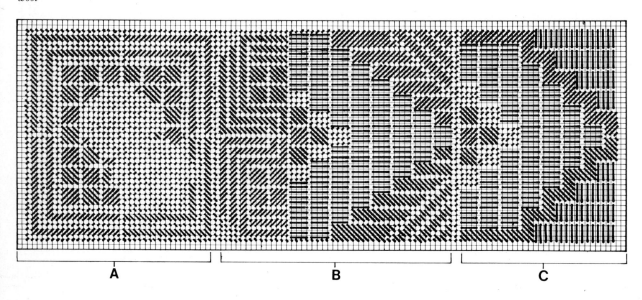

A   B   C

10 Appliqué is Fun

Appliqué really is enormous fun. It is the technique of creating patterns and designs by cutting out shapes from one type of material and fixing them in place on another. It can be used in very exciting ways for clothes (more about them in Chapter 11), cushions, pictures, etc., and is one of the quickest ways of creating really bold, large scale effects, for decorating big floor cushions for example.

What you can use
There is no limit to the variety of fabrics, printed and plain, which can be used to form designs.

Accumulate a rag bag, hoarding all suitable scraps that come your way — pattern samples, dress-making odds and ends, and remember that odd lengths of ribbons and braid can also be included in appliqué designs. Some braids, e.g. daisy-chain guipure can be cut up to make very pretty shapes. The appliqué pieces themselves can be cut from almost any kind of fabric, but firmly-woven fabrics that do not easily fray are most suitable.

Embroidery stitches can be used with appliquéd fabrics to add detail and emphasis to the basic design. But you can regard these as an optional extra because it is quite possible to build up your bold effects merely using different fabrics. Often complete motifs (flowers, etc.) can be cut from a printed dress or furnishing fabric and appliquéd into place.

Almost any fabric can be used for the background and the appliqué pieces can be sewn with a fine matching thread or you can use an embroidery thread in a contrasting colour, if the appliqué is to be attached with decorative stitches.

Several kinds of fabric can be used in one design, and this gives lots of scope for the imagination. Ideal are non-fray fabrics such as felt, though felt will not wash. You can prevent other materials from fraying by ironing on an adhesive bonded interlining to the back of the fabric before you cut out your basic shape. When your appliquéd article is going to come in for hard wear, you should take care to see that the grain of the two fabrics runs the same way. This will prevent puckering and splitting.

Using a frame

These can be useful for appliquéd work as they ensure that the background material is held taut. Small items can be worked on a tambour frame on a stand, because you need both hands free, but larger pieces will need to be mounted in a slate frame (see Chapter 1).

METHODS OF WORKING

Cutting and stitching

Felt shapes and other firm, non-fray materials can be cut out and slip-stitched into place — or you can use a more deliberately decorative kind of stitch. Alternatively, use a zig-zag stitch on a swing-needle sewing machine over the raw edges. Shapes can be held in place initially with a dab of fabric glue.

Stitching then cutting

Some fabrics fray as soon as you cut them, and in this case you should mark out your outline, and then leave a good margin around it as you cut it out. Buttonhole round the outline shape by hand (or zig-zag by machine) to secure the shape to the main fabric. Then trim off the surplus appliquéd fabric. To do this, you will need a pair of really sharp-pointed little scissors.

Blind appliqué

This is an alternative method for fabrics that fray easily, giving a neat non-conspicuous edge. Cut out your shape with a seam allowance of about $\frac{1}{4}$ in. all around. Turn the edges under and baste or tack in position. If the shape is difficult you can use a card template. When you have pressed the turnings flat, pin and slipstitch the shape into position, and remove basting. Your shape will settle down better if you have cut across corners and clipped into curves.

A variation on this method is to mark out your shape on the appliqué fabric and then to machine stitch around it for a really neat turning edge. Then cut it out, leaving the $\frac{1}{4}$ in. allowance for turning under and slipstitching (see diagrams).

WHAT YOU CAN MAKE

A large floor cushion

Designed by Sally Crowle. Floor cushions are very popular at the moment, and appliqué is the ideal way of working a bold design. Our design is very easy to make. Decide on the basic size, shape and fabric for your cushion cover. Then work out the shape and position you would like your window design, using brown paper patterns. Cut out a piece of backing fabric a little larger than these shapes and machine on to it small rectangular pieces of fabric to build up the window. Small-

1) Machine stitch round outline.
2) Cut out leaving ¼″ seam allowance.

Clipped curve

Tack in place   Slipstich

The working of these embroidered jeans is described on page 65, and the tennis shoes on page 64

A picture frame from appliqued felt

scale patterns work best. You can include some areas of plain fabric for embroidery, as shown. Stitch narrow ribbon in place to give the criss-cross window effect and conceal the joins. For an ultra quick way of making your initial patchwork you could use white adhesive nylon web which, using an iron, bonds two fabrics together.

Slip-stitch your appliquéd patchwork window panel into place on the cushion cover, making a neat turning.

Applique picture frame

Designed by Jenni Moor. You will need thick card, felt in colours of your own choice (we made the frame bright green, with grey rectangle appliquéd sections, green leaves and bright red poppies). You will also need strong fabric glue, small beads and red stranded cotton.

Cut one piece of card to the desired shape of frame (ours was 5 in. x 7 in.) and cut out the hole for the picture (1). Cut a slightly smaller piece of card for backing (2), cut a piece of card rectangular in shape about two thirds the length of the frame for its prop (3), draw round the shape of your frame card on

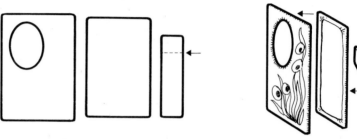

paper, and then work out your appliquéd pattern. Use this as a pattern for all pieces, cutting shapes as required. Cover prop and backing card in base colour felt. Work appliqué pattern on felt for the frame shape, before gluing into place, remembering to leave enough extra material for neat turnings and edges. Cut shapes to be appliquéd and glue lightly into position. Add decorative straight stitches for hairy stems of poppies and veins on leaves. Small black beads are used for stamens on flowers. When stitching is complete cover the frame, gluing on the underside only, to make sure the glue does not spoil the appliqué. Trim all underside corners of excess felt and glue all parts together, leaving space at the top or side to insert photograph or picture (4).

Appliqué heart motif

Designed by Su Gamson. This would be very attractive for a cushion, or for decorating clithes, or making a picture. Simply cut out circles of different coloured felts using a punch, and thread them tightly together, making a long snake-like section. This can be curved into any shape you fancy, and then stitched into place.

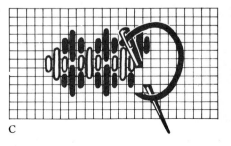

Appliqué cuff

Remember that you can use braid and ribbons to great effect in appliqué work. This attractive cuff was made by cutting out strips from an old piece of black lace from a rag bag. The resulting motifs were then secured in place with embroidery stitches in a contrasting colour: little straight stitches, and tiny cross stitches. The edges were trimmed with black net. It is possible to buy heavy braids to create a similar effect.

Small felt flowers

Designed by Su Gamson. These were made by taking layers of different coloured felts, catching them with a single stitch to a backing fabric, and then cutting round the whole lot into the desired shapes (circles, squares, crosses, etc.). These little flowers could be used to make a free-style pattern on cushions and so on, or as an attractive edging for a bolero, or stitched along a belt.

Pussy-cat picture *(Illustrated in colour on page 55)*

The ding-dong-bell pussy cat wall panel has been designed and worked in felt appliqué and embroidery by Su Gamson.

You will find the design easier to work if you make it considerably larger than the outline sketch. Refer to Chapter 12 for notes on using the grid system for enlargements.

Su used a fairly complicated selection of stitches to enrich her basic appliqué design, and diagrams for those stitches not already featured in the book are given overleaf. But this design would still be very effective worked almost entirely in felt appliqué shapes, using much simpler stitches for the embroidery effects.

Above: a cuff appliqued from old lace. Left: These small felt flowers can be used to decorate cushions or belts

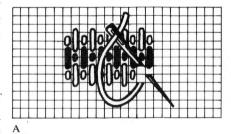

A

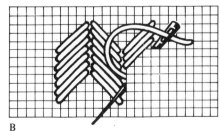

B

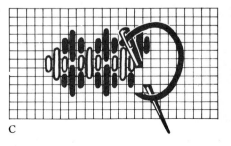

C

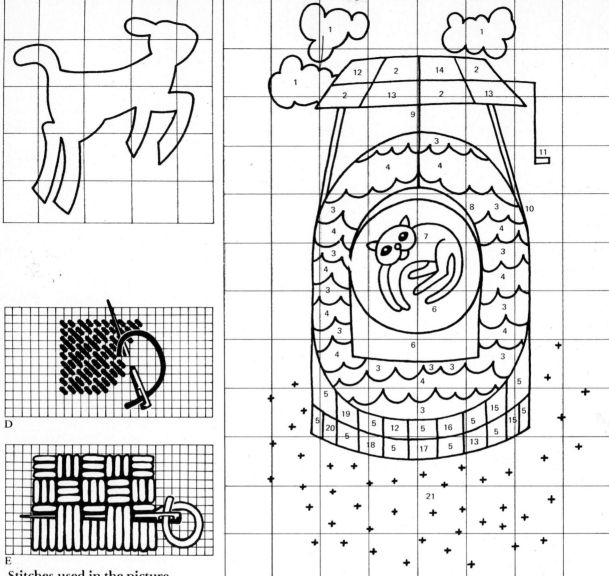

Stitches used in the picture

(all numbers in brackets refer to Chapter 2 unless stated otherwise)

1. Satin stitch clouds (11).
2. Felt slates with zig-zag straight stitch (10)
3. Felt water, stitched invisibly.
4. Satin stitched water (11).
5. Felt bricks with backstitch (2).
6. Felt bucket with cross stitched edges (Chapter 5).
7. Felt cat with straight stitch (10).
8. Handle of couched chain stitch (22 and couching).
9. Rope of chain stitch (22).
10. Well outline and roof supports in blanket stitch (19).
11. Handle in satin stitch (11).
12. Rice stitch (see Chapter 9).
13. Layers of fly stitch (21).
14. Canvas style stem stitch (see diagram B).
15. Petit point or tent stitch (see Chapter 9).
16. Hungarian stitch (see diagram C).
17. Satin stitch (11).
18. Parisian stitch (see diagram A).
19. Florence stitch (see diagram D).
20. Plaited stitch (see diagram E).
21. Mixtures of the above stitches.

Exciting but simple shirt motifs

11 Embroidery for Fashion Flair

It is top fashion today to have your clothes as highly decorated as possible, and embroidery is a quick, cheap way of adding decoration to transform a mass-produced garment into something uniquely personal. Embroidery you have done yourself will be admired wherever you go; it doesn't have to be elaborate. The simple fact that your clothes are hand-decorated in an age of machine finishes is enough to make you stand out from the crowd.

Embroidery fortunately doesn't have to be kept for girl's clothes, either . . . or to be done only by girls for that matter. The heavy shirts in the picture were designed and worked by Edward Nichols, a talented young craftsman.

You can use all the styles of embroidery this book has featured. Appliqué is good because it is so quick to do. Freestyle embroidery patterns are fun and you could start with some of the simple borders shown in Chapter 3. They would go well round the bottoms of jeans, round cuffs, down the edges of boleros and jerkins, or round the bottoms of skirts. You could also experiment with some of the motifs shown in Chapter 13. Many of these are ideal for clothes.

Take care where you place your motifs on clothes. Unless you can cover a large area with closely worked stitches, group motifs together, rather than have them scattered around. Ideal places for positioning motifs are on pockets, collars, the back of shirts, on back pockets of jeans or down the side. Choose threads and appliqué that are colour fast; clothes have to be washed some time or other, and it would be a shame for your work to be spoiled.

SOME ORIGINAL IDEAS

Embroidered tennis shoes
These were designed by Frances Challis. She pencilled in her amoeba-shaped patterns and then filled the shapes with Cretan stitch (see diagram) and lines of satin stitch with a single couching thread. The shapes on the toe-cap were painted in as the rubber made embroidery impossible, and enamel paint was used.

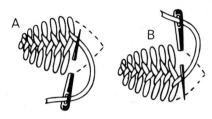

through centrally at the left-
... the lower line, needle
... the needle point,
... thread under
... shape is filled.

... Jenni Moor who
... avy blocks of satin
... e side of the jeans so
...n. You can trace the

Above: *detail of the embroidered jeans shown
in colour on page 59*

Below: *detail of art nouveau skirt. Also shown
in colour on front cover*

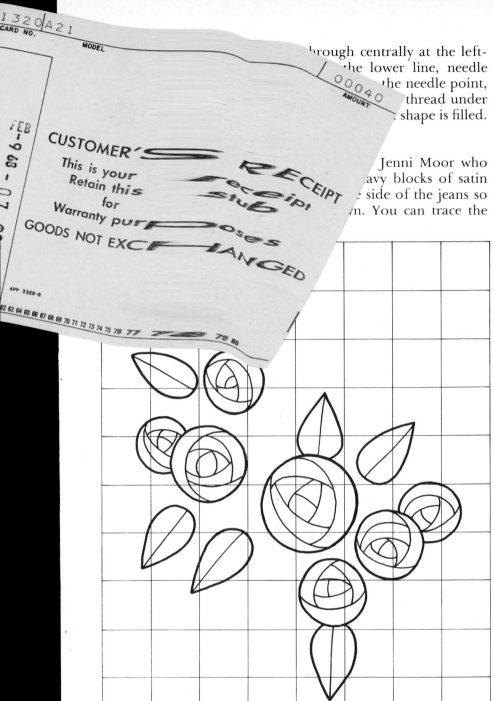

Long skirt with art nouveau pattern
Designed by Julie Daniels. Leaf motifs were cut from a printed
fabric and appliquéd on, using a machine. But they could be
applied by hand, using a neat ridge of satin stitch. The flowers
were then linked with long trailing stems of chain stitch in
pearl cotton.

Emb.-E

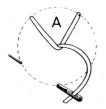
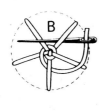

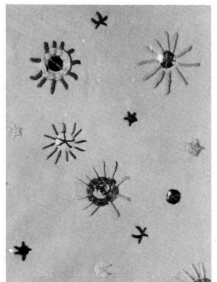

Above: *sequin centres with woven spokes*

Below: *a simple motif for a child's dress*

Panelled skirt

One panel was decorated with free style spider web stitches for the smaller motifs (see diagram), together with spoked woven motifs, an adaptation of this idea.

Spider web filling. Commence with a fly stitch to the centre of the circle as shown in A, then work two straight stitches, one on each side of the fly stitch tail, into the centre of the circle. This divides the circle into five equal sections and the 'spokes' form the foundation of the web. Weave over and under the 'spokes' until the circle is filled as at B. In drawn-thread embroidery the 'spokes' are not completely covered by the weaving. Only half the circle is filled, which gives the filling an open, lacy appearance.

Larger motifs were worked with straight stitch spokes and then woven in a similar fashion, sometimes using a contrasting thread. Take care that you always have an odd number of spokes, and decorate the centres with a sequin or button.

A child's dress

This shows how a simple motif can be repeated to create a design that fits in with the style of the garment. The stitches are simple: stem, satin and running.

Embroidered shirts
Edward Nichols has used chain stitch to create lively and unusual designs, three of which we reproduce in outline for you to copy.

Appliqué tie
A motif from a Fidelis furnishing fabric, stiffened with iron-on lining, and button-hole stitched into place, transforms a rather ordinary chain-store tie.

An appliqué jumper
A large motif was cut from a Fidelis furnishing fabric, leaving extra fabric around the edges. The motif was decorated with extra embroidery stitches and then appliquéd into place using button-hole stitch. The excess fabric was carefully trimmed off, using a small pair of sharp-pointed scissors.

Belts
Designed by Judith Standeven.
Design number 1 is a simple, repeating, geometric pattern created from triangular pieces of felt appliquéd on to the background with small, widely-spaced running stitches. The linking embroidered line is stem stitch in six strands of stranded cotton or six-strand floss.

Appliqued jumper (see page 67)

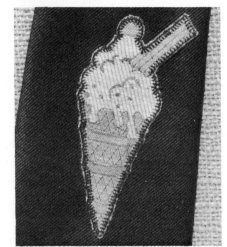

Appliqued tie (see page 67)

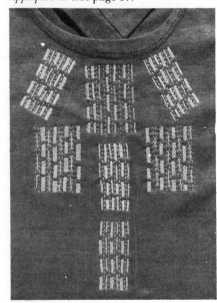

Embroidered T-shirt

Design number 2 is also simple and geometric. The background is two broad strips of contrasting colour, and the line where they join is an important part of the design. Half-oval shapes of felt are appliquéd to each side of the centre line, and the shape is completed in each case with a double line of chain stitch in contrasting colours.

Design number 3 uses herringbone stitch to create interesting shapes. The lines of herringbone, worked in three strands of stranded cotton, start very small, and then are worked gradually larger, so that the effect is of a solid line that seems to fan out.

An embroidered T-shirt *(Illustrated in colour on back cover)*
Designed by Frances Challis. The designer has created a simple effective pattern by working blocks of stem stitch, running stitch, and feather stitch. The back of the work is strengthened with fine white cotton to make a firm base for the embroidery.

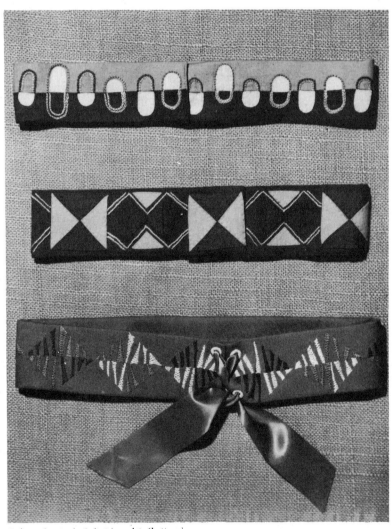

Belts 1 (centre), 2 (top) and 3 (bottom)

12 Some Notes on Working Methods

However accomplished at embroidery stitches and techniques you may be, the ultimate success of your work will depend as much on the appeal of your basic designs, as on your skill in realising them.

There is plenty of help available in the form of printed transfers and books of designs, and beginners should not hesitate to take advantage of them. There is scope for personal expression in adapting stitches, colours and fabrics to your own ideas. Adaptation is much more fun than outright copying but at the same time there is the reassurance of a well-defined starting point.

The use of decorative stitches

As has been stressed, many embroidery stitches can be used to build up non-pictorial designs as they are decorative in their own right. Borders are probably the simplest illustration of this and examples were shown in Chapters 2 and 8 but you will probably want to work out your own. It is easiest for beginners to work borders across each end of an article (e.g. a table runner) or all round the bottom of something (e.g. a skirt) as turning corners may present complications. Remember to allow for your hem (for notes on finishing off see Chapter 14), when planning the position. A fine line in pencil or lightly used ball-point pen will help to keep lines of stitches straight.

Templates for wavy lines

Flowing wavy lines can be created by tracing round large coins, or round the rim of a glass, or, of course, by using a circular template made with a compass. Study the diagram to see how you can achieve variations in the degree of curves. Using this simple guide, you can work out quite complex patterns of interlacing wavy lines, interpreting them in whichever stitches you have become proficient.

Turning corners

Sometimes you may require your border to turn a corner, and you can work out the necessary detail using a mirror — a small handbag one will do. Draw a straight section of the border on tracing paper, lay it on a flat surface and stand the mirror at 45 degrees across it, as shown in the diagram. This will reflect the

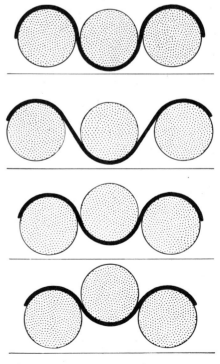

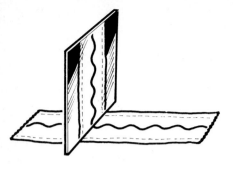

detail of the corner. Move the mirror backwards and forwards, lengthening and shortening the corner until the reflection gives the detail which seems best. When you think you have the most satisfactory corner detail, draw a pencil line across the paper along the lower edge of the mirror, and cut along this diagonal line. Reverse the paper and fit the diagonal lines together.

Using transfers

Transfers tend perhaps to be less adventurous and imaginative than one would like, but it is possible to use them effectively as with the greetings card on page 22. They come in blue, yellow or black print — yellow for use on black fabric, blue for light colours, and black for blue, green or brown. Single-impression transfers can only be used once, but multi-impression transfers can be used up to eight times (less for coarse heavy fabrics than for fine fabrics) and this is useful if you are using them to create a repeating pattern. Transfers are applied to the fabric using a hot iron — wool temperature for single impression, cotton temperature for multi-print. First of all, cut away the lettering from the transfer and use this for testing, if possible on a piece of fabric similar to your work. Lay the lettering on the fabric, shiny side down, and increase the heat of the iron slightly if the impression is not clear. When your test has proved satisfactory, place the main transfer (shiny side down) on the fabric in the required position, and fix it with pins. Apply the iron for a few seconds and remove. Carefully lift a corner of the transfer paper to check that the design has come off satisfactorily. If not, re-apply iron. Then carefully peel off the paper and, if it sticks to the fabric, run the iron over it again. Be very careful not to move either transfer or fabric or a smudged impression will result. Always embroider to the outside edge of a transfer line so that the embroidery stitches cover the transfer ink.

Using tracing paper for transferring designs

For more imaginative designs you will want to apply motifs from books or magazines or other sources to your fabric — motifs similar to those presented in Chapters 2 and 13 for example. Buy special tracing paper for preference, or use ordinary kitchen greaseproof paper (butcher paper). Trace off your design. Then apply it to the fabric, using dress maker's carbon paper, which is much cleaner to use than ordinary typewriting carbon paper — though this can be used at a pinch. Work on a hard firm surface and pin your tracing paper, with the carbon paper under it, into position so that it doesn't move. Draw over all lines with a sharp pointed pencil or the point of a knitting needle. If no carbon paper is available, you can get fair results by using a soft pencil for the tracing and then laying your pencilled tracing face downwards on the fabric and going over the design (which will be reversed, of course) with a hard pencil, pressing as hard as possible.

There are other methods of transferring designs from paper to fabric. You can, for example, trace the outline on tissue paper and then tack the outline on to the fabric through the tissue paper, which is then removed, but beginners may find this too slow and therefore discouraging.

Changing the scale of a pattern

You may well need to enlarge or reduce a motif. You can for example create an attractive all-over pattern by enlarging and reducing the same simple motif, all over an area such as a cushion cover. You can do this by drawing a squared grid over a square of rectangular area which encloses your original design (or you can do it on tracing paper placed over the top if you cannot mark the original). Alternatively you can reproduce the original design on paper ready printed with small squares. Number the squares down the side and letter them along the top. Now draw out a grid with larger (enlarging) or smaller (reducing) squares on a separate piece of paper, and number and letter them in the same way. If you want to make your design twice as big, make your second set of squares twice as big as the first and so on.

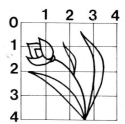

You may find working out the scale of enlargement a bit tricky. In this case draw a diagonal (see diagram) through the rectangle or square enclosing the design on your original drawing. Extend the diagonal AB until it represents the diagonal of a rectangle or square that would enclose a design of the required larger or smaller size (line AC in the diagram). Draw a line CD parallel to the top of the original square/rectangle. Extend AE to meet CD. To determine the size of squares for your enlarging grid, divide CD into the same number of parts you had for your first grid for the rectangle/square AEBX.

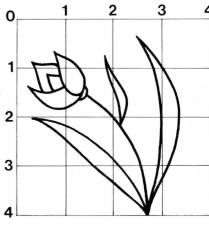

Redraw the design on to the second grid, marking on it first of all the points where the design crosses the lines of the first grid (using the letters and numbers as a guide) and then joining up these points.

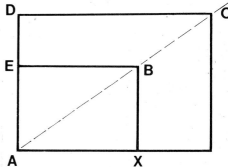

Using paper patterns

When making articles from scratch, however simple the shape may seem, it is a good plan to cut out a pattern in brown paper or newspaper to make sure the idea works before you cut the fabric irrevocably. Allow for turnings and tack them in place and try out the paper pattern as if it were the finished article — to see how the size of a cushion, for example, will blend with your chair or sofa, or how a set of mats will fit a table. Such a lot depends on correct proportions.

To help decide where to position motifs, you can move your traced design (or cut-out paper shape) around until you arrive at the best position.

13 Simple Motifs to Copy or Adapt

By now you are probably quite proficient at stitching, and may be looking around for interesting designs. Perhaps you want to create your own, but in case you feel slightly at a loss, here is a good selection of basic outlines which you can interpret as you like, using the grid system to enlarge or reduce (see Chapter 12). We have stitched up some of them to illustrate their potential. All stitch numbers refer to Chapter 2.

Two suns. The two suns show different ways of treating the same shape. The one has a yellow circle of fabric overcast (7) on to red rick-rack, and then heavily couched in a trellis pattern (31) with tiny centres of straight stitch (10). The other is quite simply cut from orange and yellow felt, slip-stitched down.

Two flowers. The two flowers are also an identical motif given two different looks. The one is mainly appliquéd, with the pink petal shape held in place with blanket stitch (19) and the flat centre slip-stitched on and decorated with French knots (28). The stem is two lines of stem stitch (3) filled in with tiny crosses, and the appliquéd flat leaves, slip stitched down, and have feather stitch (20) veining. The embroidered flower has petals outlined in stem stitch (3), filled in with shaded long and short stitch (12). The stem is chain stitch (22) with leaf outlines in stem (3), filled in thick smooth satin stitch (11). The little liquorice allsort cube is appliquéd from felt shapes slip stitched down, with blanket stitch (19) round the edge, three lines of stem (3) in the middle, and a line of stem plus little crosses at the top.

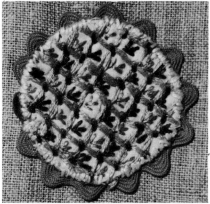

14 Finishing Off

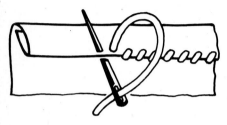

Many of the ideas in previous chapters are for applying embroidery to things you already have — clothes, for example, or linen. If you are feeling more ambitious, however, you may want to make your own articles from scratch, particularly when you are planning your embroidery design around a special kind of fabric. Here are some ways of finishing them off, and a few other tips.

Always work your embroidery before making up, so that you are stitching a single piece of fabric. On fabrics that fray easily, it is necessary to overcast the edge with large stitches before starting. When your embroidered article is completed, the edges will need finishing off. There are various simple ways of doing this.

A SIMPLE HEM

After making a double fold, pinning if necessary, work it in hemming stitch, pulling the needle through the material one thread from the edge of the hem and then starting it through the fold so that it comes out 2 threads above the edge of the fold.

A DECORATIVE STITCH AND HEM

This works well for fine fabrics. A line of decorative stitching, e.g. feather stitch (Chapter 2, 20), is used to conceal the stitches of a fine hem. The trick is to work the decorative stitch first on a single thickness of fabric and then to make your fine hem on the wrong side, making sure the embroidery conceals the hem stitches. Blanket stitch (Chapter 2, 19) can be worked along finished edges. A second line can be worked to fit into the first to make a heavier border. Knot stitch is another used for edging — sometimes called Antwerp stitch. Bring the thread through from the back of the fabric and work a single loose buttonhole stitch. Pass the needle behind the loop of the stitch and over the working thread as shown in diagram. Space the stitches about $4\frac{1}{4}$ in. apart. This edging is very useful for handkerchiefs or lingerie. Several rows, using a different colour for each row, make a lacy edging. The stitches of the second and following rows are worked over the loops between the stitches of the previous row.

DRAWN-THREAD FINISHES

Simple drawn-thread techniques can be used to create attractive hems.

Hemstitch

First of all, work out the depth of hem you would like and add on a small allowance for turnings. Then withdraw the required number of threads. Do not withdraw the threads right across fabric, but only to form a square or rectangle. Cut the threads at the centre and withdraw gradually outwards on each side to within the hem measurement, leaving a sufficient length of thread at the corners in order to darn the ends invisibly. Turn back the hem to the space of the drawn threads, mitre corners (see below) and baste or tack. Bring the working thread, which can be a contrasting colour, out two threads down from the space of drawn threads, through the folded hem at the right-hand side. Pass the needle behind four loose threads, bringing the needle out two threads down through all the folds of the hem in readiness for next stitch. The number of threads may be varied to suit the fabric or design.

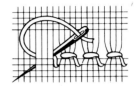

Ladder Hemstitch

This stitch is worked in the same way as hemstitch, with the hemstitch being worked along both edges of the space of drawn threads. Hemstitch and ladder hemstitch may be worked on fine linen or even-weave linen.

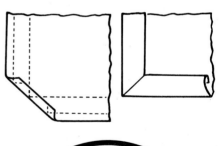

Zig-Zag Hemstitch

This variation is worked as hemstitch, but there must be an even number of threads in each group of loose threads caught together in the first row. In the second row, the groups are divided in half, so that each group is composed of half the number of threads from one group and half from the adjacent group. A half group starts and ends the second row.

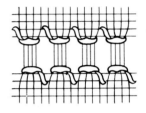

MITRING CORNERS

A mitre is a fold used to achieve smooth shaping at a corner. To mitre a corner on a hem, fold and press the hem, open the hem and fold the corner inwards on the inner fold line. Cut off the corner, leaving a small seam allowance (Fig. A). Refold hem, slip stitch the diagonal line of the mitre, and hem (Fig. B).

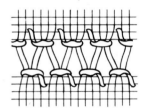

THE USE OF BIAS BINDING

This is very useful for curved edges, such as round tablecloths or bibs, or for heavy fabrics where a hem would be unattractively bulky. First, lay the binding on the fabric, edge to edge, right sides together, and stitch along the top fold of the binding, stretching the binding slightly. Then, turn the binding over to the wrong side of the fabric and slip stitch along the folded edge of the binding.

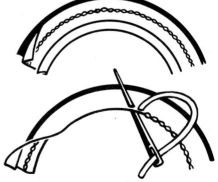

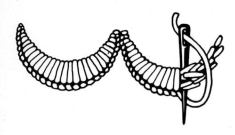

BUTTONHOLE AND SCALLOPS

Buttonhole stitch (Chapter 2, 19) can be used over either a raw edge or a finished hem (see diagram) and is very effective combined with scallops. Work small slanting stitches from the top part of the scallop, increasing and curving them round the bottom. Long running stitches can be worked as padding.

Make a template for scallops from a piece of stiff card (the back of a cereal packet will do). Draw two parallel lines fairly close together on the card. Lay a large coin (or glass, or small plate) between them and trace a scalloped line moving the coin along as many times as you need to complete your template. It's best to make shallow scallops because deep points between them are more tricky to work and do not look as satisfactory. It is easiest to work with a shortish template, moving it along as necessary.

FRINGES

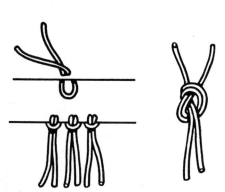

Fringes are old-fashioned but, like so many old styles, are enjoying a current fashion revival. You can make them by using the threads of the fabric you are working on.

Make sure the raw edge of your work is completely straight and then withdraw one or two threads about 1 in. from the edge, the distance depending on the depth you would like for your fringe. Along the line of the top of the withdrawn thread work, hemstitch (see above) along the inside edge, binding threads in groups of three or four and taking up two threads of the main fabric. When you have finished working the hemstitch, you can pull out all the outer threads to make the fringe.

Alternatively, you can add a fringe of another thread — perhaps in a contrasting colour and texture. This can be particularly effective on heavier fabrics.

Cut threads into lengths twice the depth you have chosen for your fringe. Then, working with small groups of threads, (you will need to experiment here, but six is a good guide and the number must be even if you intend to knot (see below), fold the lengths in half and use a crochet hook to draw the looped ends through the edge of the fabric. Thread the ends through the loops and pull tight.

For a distinctive effect, you can knot your fringe into a diamond pattern (see diagram).

WASHING AND CLEANING

Some embroidery (e.g. canvas work) will require dry cleaning. But if fabric is washable and threads are colour-fast, washing is possible, taking great care and always washing by hand, each item separately. Make sure your powder (pure soap) is thoroughly dissolved, rinse several times, and do not boil, soak or bleach. For deep-coloured and heavily embroidered fabrics, rinse over and over again until the water comes completely clear. To absorb excess moisture, roll the embroidery in a clean dry towel, and do not allow it to get too dry before ironing. Use a hot iron on a padded ironing surface, pulling the fabric to shape as you go along. Iron linen on the wrong side until dry. Dry cleaning is best for all articles with a substantial amount of embroidery, although it is not practical for table linen and clothes which require frequent cleaning. This should be remembered when choosing designs for these items. All heavy fabrics — especially wool and synthetics — should be dry-cleaned, as should all canvas work, feltwork and appliqué.

15 Embroidery, Free Style

This is the last chapter in the book and it seems appropriate to end with something imaginative and adventurous.

The designs here have all been worked without a great deal of careful initial planning. The embroiderers had a rough idea of what they wanted to achieve, a good stitching knowledge, plus a plentiful supply of beads, braids, etc. Then they started, and just let the panels develop in their own way. This can be great fun, and maybe these illustrations will inspire you sufficiently to have a go if by now you should have plenty of stitching know-how and confidence.

Beads on rich fabrics
Exciting panels can be made by stitching all sorts of different kinds of beads on to luxurious fabrics — in this case velvet and crêpe.

Chain stitch on velvet
Thick loops of chain stitch in bright colours were worked to cover an area of red velvet.

Chain stitch worked on velvet

Bead designs stitched on to fabric

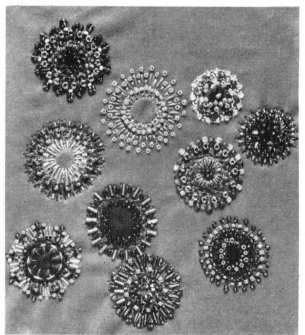
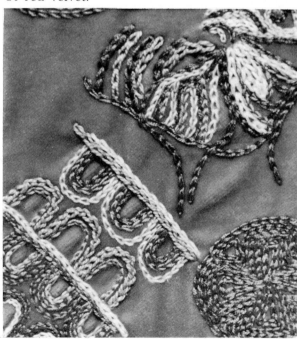

Flower outline filled in with random stitches

The outline of a five petalled flower was sketched in freehand and outlined in chain, stem and herringbone stitches. Then the centre was filled in with a random assortment of lazy daisy, french knots, chain and stem stitches etc. with sequins, and daisy motifs cut from braid and appliquéd. The pattern was made up as the worker went along, and the result is a delightful informality, not at all difficult to achieve.

Wool handbag

A design of straight stitch leaves and flowers, with the stitches all going different ways, was evolved by the embroiderer, Jill Harding, as she went along. She used up all the odd bits of wool she had in the house and this type of working is simple to copy.

A free-style embroidered flower (left)

Straight stitch leaves and flowers used for a handbag (below)

THE LAST WORD

I hope you have got as much fun out of this book as we have had in putting it together. Once you know a little bit about embroidery you'll find that there are no end of ways you can use your new found skills.

So happy stitching and good luck!

Index

Alphabets:
application of 39
initials 42
method of working 40
monograms 42
stitches for 39
Appliqué:
beginnings and
materials 57
methods of working 58
things to make 58-61
Apron in cross-stitch
Basic equipment 5
Basic stitches 10
Bead embroidery 78
Beginnings and
materials 5-9
Belt, canvaswork 56
Belt, embroidered 67
Bias binding 75
Borders:
braid 18
daisy 20
flower 20
leaf 18
Canvas work (see
Needlepoint)
blocking and cleaning 47
canvas meshes 46
choosing canvas 46
hints on working 47
materials and
equipment 46, 47
stitches:
bricking 48
Byzantine 49
chequer 49
continental 48
Florentine 49
half cross 48
rice 49
Scottish 49
star 49
tent 48
things to make 50-56
Chenille needles 8
Child's dress 66
Choosing fabrics 5
Cleaning embroidery 76
Clothing embroidery:
belt 67
child's dress 66
jeans 65
jumper 67
long skirt 65
panelled skirt 66
shirt 67
T-shirt 68
tennis shoes 64
Counted thread:
fabrics and
materials 26-28
method of working 28
types of designs 26
Crewel work:
materials, equipment 8
stitches 38
Cross stitch
embroidery 35
Cross Stitch patterns:
apron 36
border 34
table runner 35
Cuff in appliqué 61

Drawn thread work 75
Edges for finishing:
bias bound 75
buttonholed 76
fringed 76
hemmed 74
hem-stitched 75
scalloped 76
Embroidery techniques:
appliqué 57
counted thread 28
canvas work 46
needlepoint 46
gingham, on, 17
folk embroidery 26
wool 38
Enlarging patterns 71
Equipment for
embroidery 5-9
Evenweave fabric 5
Fabrics 5, 6, 26
Fabrics which fray 74
Fashion embroidery:
belt 67
child's dress 66
handbag 79
jeans 65
jumper 67
long skirt 65
panelled skirt 66
T-shirt 68
tennis shoes 64
Felt appliqué, flowers 61
Finishing techniques 74
Five basic stitches 10
Floor cushion, appliqué 58
Florentine embroidery 49
Frames:
method of working
with 9
preparing to work 9
sizes and types 9
Fringed edges 76
Free-style embroidery 78
Gingham embroidery 17
Greetings card 22
Guide to stitches 10-16
Handbag 79
Hemmed edges 74
Hemstitch 75
Hem-stitching 75
Initials and monograms 39-43
Jacobean embroidery 38
Jeans decoration 65
Jumper 67
Keeping work clean 6
Letters 39
Linen for embroidery 6
Materials 5-9
Mitred corners 75
Monograms and
initials 39-43
Motifs to adapt 72
Necktie 67
Needlepoint: (see canvas
work)
blocking and cleaning 47
canvas meshes 26
choosing canvas 46
hints on working 47
materials and equipment 46
stitches:
bricking 48
Byzantine 49
chequer 49
continental 48
Florentine 49
half cross 48

rice 49
Scottish 49
star 49
tent 48
things to make 50-56
Needles 8
Panel, Four seasons 51
Paper patterns 71
Patterns and motifs:
alphabet letters 39
animals 67
art deco 21
art nouveau 65
belt design, canvas
work 56
butterfly 22
cross stitch designs 34
cuff in appliqué 61
fir tree 73
five petalled flower 79
flower border 20
flowers in felt 61
Four seasons panel 51
heart, in appliqué 60
interlacing 44
Jacobean design 38
leaf border 18
leaves and flowers 65
leaves and flowers,
wool 79
Maltese cross 45
Portuguese border 45
raised chain border 45
rose and leaf 65
striped woven border 45
two flowers 72
two suns 72
Picture frame, appliqué 60
Pre-shrinking fabrics 6
Pressing work 6
Pussy-cat picture 61
Reducing patterns 71
Ring frame 9
Sampler 24
Scalloped edges 76
Shirt 67
Shoes 64
Shrinking fabrics 6
Silk thread 8
Six-stranded floss 7
Skirt, long 65
Skirt, panelled 66
Slate frame 9
Soft embroidery thread 7
Special effects 44
Stitches:
back 11
back (counted thread) 29
blanket 14
buttonhole 14
cable 11
cable chain 15
chain 14
chevron 16
couching 16
cross 28
detached chain 15
double cross 28
double running 30
feather 14
fern 16
fishbone 13
flat 13
fly 14
four sided 32
Florence 62
French knots 15
herringbone 14

hemstitch 75
Holbein 30
honeycomb 32
Hungarian 62
interlacing 45
Jacobean couching 16
laced running 11
ladder 44
ladder hemstitch 75
lazy daisy 15
leaf 13
long-legged cross 29
long and short 12
open fishbone 13
open chain 15
overcast 12
padded satin stitch 43
Parisian 62
Pekinese 11
plaited stitch 62
Portuguese 45
ringed back 30
Roumanian 13
Roumanian couching 16
running 11
satin 12
satin (counted thread) 12
scroll 12
seeding 16
spider's web filling 66
split 12
stem 11
straight 12
trailing 12
trellis 16
two-colour chain 15
vandyke 44
wave 30
whipped back 30
zig-zag hemstitch 75
Stranded cotton 7
T-shirt 68
Table linen 21
Table napkin 21
Table runner 35
Tambour frame 9
Threads for embroidery:
crewel wool 8
pearl cotton 7
six-stranded floss 7
soft embroidery cotton 7
stranded cotton 7
silk 8
tapestry wool 7
Threads, evenweave fabric 5
Tracing technique 70
Transferring designs 70, 71
Transfers 70
Turning corners 69
Use of stitches 69
Using templates 69
Valentine card 22
Velvet embroidery 78
Wool embroidery 38, 79
Working methods:
enlarging patterns 71
finishing; bias binding 75
buttonholed edges 76
drawn thread 75
hemmed 74
fringed 76
mitred corners 75
scalloped edges 76
reducing patterns 71
transferring designs 70, 71
Washing and cleaning 76